Les Murray

CONTEMPORARY WORLD WRITERS

SERIES EDITOR   JOHN THIEME

ALREADY PUBLISHED IN THE SERIES

Peter Carey   BRUCE WOODCOCK

Kazuo Ishiguro   BARRY LEWIS

Timothy Mo   ELAINE YEE LIN HO

Toni Morrison   JILL MATUS

Alice Munro   CORAL ANN HOWELLS

Ngugi wa Thiong'o   PATRICK WILLIAMS

Salman Rushdie   CATHERINE CUNDY

Derek Walcott   JOHN THIEME

Les Murray

STEVEN MATTHEWS

Manchester University Press
Manchester and New York

distributed exclusively in the USA by Palgrave

Published by Manchester University Press
Oxford Road, Manchester M13 9NR, UK
and Room 400, 175 Fifth Avenue, New York, NY 10010, USA
www.manchesteruniversitypress.co.uk

Distributed exclusively in the USA by
Palgrave, 175 Fifth Avenue, New York NY 10010, USA

Distributed exclusively in Canada by
UBC Press, University of British Columbia, 2029 West Mall,
Vancouver, BC, Canada V6T 1Z2

British Library Cataloguing-in-Publication Data
A catalogue record for this book is available from the British Library

Library of Congress Cataloging-in-Publication Data
A catalog record for this book is available from the Library of Congress

ISBN 13: 978 0 7190 5448 8

First published by Manchester University Press 2001

First digital paperback edition published 2008

Printed by Lightning Source

For Elleke

Contents

Series editor's foreword

Contemporary World Writers is an innovative series of authorita-
tive introductions to a range of culturally diverse contemporary
writers from outside Britain and the United States, or from 'minor-
ity' backgrounds within Britain or the United States. In addition to
providing comprehensive general introductions, books in the series
also argue stimulating original theses, often but not always related
to contemporary debates in post-colonial studies.

The series locates individual writers within their specific cultural contexts, while recognising that such contexts are themselves
invariably a complex mixture of hybridised influences. It aims to
counter tendencies to appropriate the writers discussed into the
canon of English or American literature or to regard them as 'other'.

Each volume includes a chronology of the writer's life, an introductory section on formative contexts and intertexts, discussion of
all the writer's major works, a bibliography of primary and second-
ary works and an index. Issues of racial, national and cultural
identity are explored, as are gender and sexuality. Books in the
series also examine writers' use of genre, particularly ways in which
Western genres are adapted or subverted and 'traditional' local
forms are reworked in a contemporary context.

Contemporary World Writers aims to bring together the
theoretical impulse which currently dominates post-colonial studies
and closely argued readings of particular authors' works, and by so
doing to avoid the danger of appropriating the specifics of particular
texts into the hegemony of totalising theories.

Abbreviations

Unless otherwise stated, all quotations from Murray's poetry in the book are taken from the 1998 edition of *Collected Poems*, published in Britain by Carcanet Press.

The following abbreviations are used in the text to indicate quotation from other collections of Murray's poetry and prose:

BSF   *The Boys Who Stole the Funeral*
CV   *Conscious and Verbal*
DFF   *Dog Fox Field*
DM   *The Daylight Moon*
ER   *Ethnic Radio*
FN   *Fredy Neptune*
IT   *The Ilex Tree*
LCL   *Lunch and Counter Lunch*
PAE   *Poems Against Economics*
PIF   *Persistence in Folly*
PM   *The Peasant Mandarin*
PT   *The Paperbark Tree*
WC   *The Weatherboard Cathedral*
WF   *A Working Forest*

I am grateful to Robert Crawford and to Les Murray for their help in obtaining some of the materials discussed in this book.

Chronology

1938   Leslie Allan Murray born at Nabiac, New South Wales, 17 October. Baptized in Bunyah.

1948–50   Attends Bulby Brush Public School.

1951   Briefly attends Wyong High School. Mother, Miriam Pauline née Arnall, dies of miscarriage, 19 April.

1952–54   Attends Nabiac Central School.

1955–56   Attends Taree High School. First attempts to write poetry in late 1956.

1957–59   Enrols at Sydney University for Arts degree. Edits university literary magazines with Geoffrey Lehmann. Leaves Presbyterian Church of his upbringing, and displays first interest in Roman Catholicism.

1960–61   Drops out of university and hitch-hikes around Australia. First literary prominence outside university, as poems are published in *Bulletin*.

1962   Marries Valerie Gina Morelli, 29 September.

1963–67   Works as scientific and technical translator in Western European languages at Australian National University, Canberra.

1963   First child, Christina Miriam, born.

1964   Baptized and received into Roman Catholic Church.

1965   Son Daniel Allan born. *The Ilex Tree*, a book of poetry co-written with Lehmann, published by Australian National University Press. Wins Grace Leven Prize.

	Attends Commonwealth Arts Festival Poetry Conference in Cardiff, Wales, and subsequently travels in Europe.
1967	Moves with family, first to Penarth, Wales, and then to Culloden, Scotland.
1968	Receives Commonwealth Literary Fund grant for six months. Travels with family in Europe before return to Australia. Unemployed.
1969	Completes BA. First solo book, *The Weatherboard Cathedral*, published by Angus and Robertson.
1970	Returns to Canberra to work in Prime Minister's Department. Promised Federal funding to edit the first anthology of Aboriginal poetry; funding withdrawn without notice. Wins Cook Bicentennial Prize for Poetry.
1971	Moves back to Sydney, and buys house in Chatswood area. Divides time between Sydney and home at Bunyah until 1986. Becomes freelance writer.
1972	Three-year writer's fellowship. *Poems Against Economics* published.
1973–80	Joint editor of *Poetry Australia* (issues 66–73).
1974	Daughter Clare Louisa born. Secures forty-acre block of land at Bunyah. Attends Struga Poetry Festival, Macedonia. *Lunch and Counter Lunch* published. Wins National Book Council Prize.
1976	*Selected Poems: The Vernacular Republic* published. Wins C.J. Dennis Memorial Prize for 'Buladelah-Taree Holiday Song Cycle'.
1977	*Ethnic Radio* published. Speaks on republicanism in Sydney Town Hall.
1978	Fourth child, Alexander Joseph Cecil, born. Selection of prose, *The Peasant Mandarin*, published. Becomes poetry manuscript reader for Angus and Robertson.
1980	Tours Fiji, the United States, and Canada. Verse novel, *The Boys Who Stole the Funeral*, published. Wins Grace Leven Prize.

1981   In Edinburgh on Scottish–Australian Writers Exchange
            Fellowship scheme; writer-in-residence at University
            of Stirling.

1982   Fifth child, Peter Benedict, born. *The Vernacular
            Republic* published by Canongate, Edinburgh. Writer-
            in-residence at University of New South Wales.

1983   *The People's Otherworld* published. Wins National
            Book Council Prize. *The Vernacular Republic*
            published by Persea in New York.

1984   Writer-in-residence at Sydney University. Wins Austra-
            lian Literary Society Gold Medal and New South Wales
            Premier's Award for *The People's Otherworld*. Selection
            of prose, *Persistence in Folly*, published.

1985   Wins Christopher Brennan Award of Australian
            Writers and Canada-Australia Literary Prize. *The
            Australian Year*, with photographs by Peter Solness
            and others, published. Tours Canada and Great Britain.
            Plays car thief in film *I Own the Racecourse*.

1986   Returns to live at Bunyah. Tours Great Britain, as he
            has every year subsequently. *New Oxford Book of
            Australian Verse* and *Collins-Dove Anthology of
            Australian Religious Poetry* published. *Selected Poems*
            published by Carcanet, Manchester.

1987   Brief tour of India. *The Daylight Moon* published and
            becomes Poetry Book Society Choice in Great Britain.

1988   *The Daylight Moon* wins National Poetry Award.
            Poem, 'Tin Wash Dish', wins ABC [Australian Broad-
            casting Commission] Bicentennial Prize. Suffers return
            of depressive illness which had earlier appeared during
            study for BA at Sydney University.

1989   Becomes Literary Editor of *Quadrant* magazine. Made
            Officer in the Order of Australia; awarded inaugural
            Australian Creative Fellowship.

1990   *Dog Fox Field* published; wins Grace Leven Prize. Prose
            collection *Blocks and Tackles*.

1991   Resigns as poetry manuscript reader for Angus and
            Robertson. *Collected Poems* published by Carcanet;

American collected poems published as *The Rabbiter's Bounty* by Farrar Straus & Giroux, alongside *The Boys Who Stole the Funeral.*

1992   Daughter Christina marries. *Dog Fox Field* appears in the United States. *The Paperbark Tree*, selected prose for British market, published by Carcanet. *Translations from the Natural World* published in Australia, the United States and Britain.

1993   *Translations* wins New South Wales and Victoria Premier's Prizes, and National Book Council Banjo Award. First book of verse novel which became *Fredy Neptune* published in Britain by *PN Review*. Also appears in *Adelaide Review*. Begins 'Our Man in Bunyah' column in *Independent Monthly* (runs until 1996).

1994   *Collected Poems*, updated edition, published by Heinemann in Australia. *Fivefathers*, a selection of twentieth-century writing by five earlier Australian poets, published by Carcanet.

1995   Father, Cecil, dies. Emergence from depression begins after writing poem 'Burning Want'.

1996   German translation of selection of Murray's poetry published. *Subhuman Redneck Poems* published by Duffy and Snellgrove, New South Wales, and Carcanet. Liver abscess nearly kills Murray, but recovery brings also final lifting of depression.

1997   *Subhuman Redneck Poems* awarded T.S. Eliot Prize and published in the United States by Farrar Straus & Giroux. *A Working Forest*, updated selection of prose for Australian audience, published by Duffy and Snellgrove. Memoir, *Killing the Black Dog*, published by Federation Press, New South Wales.

1998   Verse novel, *Fredy Neptune*, published by Duffy and Snellgrove and Carcanet. *New Selected Poems* also published by Duffy and Snellgrove.

1999   *Fredy Neptune* published in the United States. Murray awarded Queen's Gold Medal for Poetry, at suggestion of Ted Hughes. *The Quality of Sprawl: Thoughts about Australia,* published by Duffy and Snellgrove.

2000   *Learning Human: Poems* published by Farrar Straus & Giroux.

1

Contexts and intertexts

In the opening poem of his 1999 collection, *Conscious and Verbal*, Les Murray describes a portrait-in-progress of himself, a portrait in which he is pictured floating along a shadowy river in a little boat without any visible form of propulsion. Rather, he seems to be moving the boat along 'with speech', steering it 'with my gaze':

> In the middle of the river are cobweb cassowary trees
> of the South Pacific, and on the far shore rise
> dark hills of the temperate zone. To these, at this
> moment in the painting's growth, my course is slant
> but my eye is on them. To relax, to speak European. (9)

Suddenly, in these closing lines of the poem, the generational, historical and human cost of such seemingly easeful aesthetics is revealed. Murray is braced between two worlds, ever alert to the lowering presence of the temperate north – against which his progress is measured but recalcitrant – whilst also appreciating the flora of the Southern tropics. The impression might be momentary, but it allows a delight in the motive power of a speech inflected by this dual habitat. And yet, in the poem's final sentence, that assurance in the 'course' is revealed for what it is: the result of a history of colonization which is, when fully at its ease, deaf to the resistances of the local terrain. In this, Murray pictures himself captured by the lived, and linguistic, history of his white settler ancestors in the country. For, as the theorist of Australian spatial history, Paul Carter, has averred along similar lines, 'any orientation to the new environment depends initially on finding resemblances between it and the home left behind ... the very possibility of comparison implies a conceptual vocabulary which can be transported from one place to another.'[1]

This closing sentence of Murray's poem 'Amanda's Painting', therefore, tellingly registers the poet's alertness also to the continuing dangers of a history of comparison when viewing the landscape of Australia, and the latter-day individual's place within it. The language which is used to describe that positioning, and which carries the double-sensed but vulnerable 'little craft' bearing the poet forward, is one imposed upon this habitat. Murray in mid-river is consciously enacting a version of that 'double aspect' which the poet Judith Wright famously identified as a preoccupation in Australian poetry, caught between 'the reality of exile' and 'the reality of newness and freedom' offered by the country.[2] Yet Murray implies that to 'relax' into that state is to perpetuate something of the colonizer's allegiances and blind history of brutality. The final sentence here seems to imply that the betwixt-and-between position, in which he finds himself in the painting, is one that he must consistently question and seek to propel himself beyond. The impression formed 'at this / moment in the painting's growth' might be transformed into something else, and a greater distinctiveness from the forming European vision and consciousness be eventually gained. This would be a distinctiveness in which the tragic inheritance of the past can be itself moved beyond in a more accepting future.

Murray has done more perhaps than any other recent Australian writer in seeking to define the nature of an emergent and separate national consciousness, one in which the links with Europe can be properly acknowledged and the brutal history of colonization can be exposed, but also one freed from both of these ties. To this end, he has been a cunning writer in the Joycean manner. He has adopted and adapted styles of writing, and taken up various strains of cultural material available to him in Australia, into his work, in conscious dialogue with developing debates over the nature of the country's post-colonial nationhood. Within this, he has often suggested surprising, and perhaps questionable, parallels between aspects of the different cultures in the country, but always in a wily and often wry way which seeks to move the debate onwards. From quite early in his career, he sought, for instance, to experiment with versions of Aboriginal narrative and celebration, whilst at the same time, through the continuing poems about his travels in Europe, reflecting on his and the majority of Australians' particular heritage.

All the time, however, the course of his career has remained 'slant'. It is one not easily assimilable, in its own constant adoption of new manners and styles, to any one established version of national or literary tradition. That sense of the momentary, of onward propulsion through language, which is so well captured in 'Amanda's Painting', might stand as representative of Murray's approach to his own writing, which has always been (and often contentiously so) keyed to the varying shifts of climate in Australia's recent history. To this extent, he has been a significant voice in propelling the political and cultural debates in his own country, persistently altering the 'slant' of his work in order to challenge any new complacency within the presumed political and social consensus.

Contentiously, Murray has not shirked the need to adopt potentially objectionable masks and poses, which, however, remain ever aware of the dangers of arrogance and self-aggrandisement in the kind of bardic pose presumed in the above poem. He can introduce a collection of his prose writings for an English audience, for instance, by proclaiming that 'Throughout this book, readers will encounter the debris and discarded maps of wars I have been conscripted to fight in', and include amongst those 'wars' one 'against the police-minded ideological rectitudes which have so largely captured the spirit and culture of my time' (*PT*, 7–8). The calculated provocation of this, and of similar statements by Murray, is not something I wish to underplay here, whilst also not wishing to underplay the political and social origin of such deliberate affronts. In these paragraphs from his introduction, Murray makes clear that he feels that he has fought such wars 'now alongside, now in distant parallel with mainly black and Celtic allies'. He consistently takes his perspective, in other words, from those who have formed the oppressed and ignored segments of his country's population – the Aborigines, and the descendants of the transportees or economic exiles who continue to form the poorest part of the white population. This despite the fact that, of course, he has moved beyond the circumstances of his own upbringing, and those of his ancestors, by taking up the different trade of writer.

His work aims to counter, in other words, the kinds of partial presumption and relegation in even highly sophisticated accounts of the historical and cultural position of those with his immigrant ancestry. It is clear, for example, from Ania Loomba's account of the particular intercultural hybridity in Australia (as well as in New Zealand and Canada), that 'White settlers were historically the agents of colonial rule, and their own subsequent development … does not simply align them with other colonised peoples. No matter what their differences with the mother country, white populations here were not subject to the genocide … felt by the indigenous population.'[3] Yet Murray would claim that such statements occlude the class differences between colonial governors and the economic migrants who formed his own forebears – with those who, even within his celebratory seasonal sequence 'The Idyll Wheel', are felt to have plucked despairingly 'The Misery Cord' (297). His sense of fellow-feeling with the Aborigines ('allies') is one countermining assertion against this kind of blindness. Murray's attacks on all forms of right-thinking conformism and state authority ('the police') have their origin in, and derive their effectiveness from, the anger which was generated from within his family's history. The complex denials, disadvantages, embarrassments and disinheritance amidst which he grew up led him to seek alliances, when imaginatively seeking to forge the conscience of his nation, with those in similar plights to his own.

Paul Kane has argued that, from the early days of written poetry in Australia, all poets saw themselves as having to establish a personalized cultural background for their work because of the newness of their country:

the process of establishing oneself as a poet was insepar-
able from establishing poetry in Australia. The double
burden of originating oneself and originating a tradition
... was understood and accepted by the most ambitious
and talented of poets.[4]

Murray's work shows how the 'burden of originating oneself'
takes various and complex forms, in which the self gained at any
one point is always at the cost of other ways of being. He was to
register the complexities of this multiple viewpoint when
prefacing a 1984 collection of his prose pieces:

My own suspicion is that I am taking part in an experiment, one which I am not aware that I designed, to discover
whether it is possible any longer to be an individual in
Australia (*PIF*, 3).

That equivocal sense of giftedness, the troubling dangers
and excitements of 'talent', resonates across all of Murray's
work, down to the long verse novel, *Fredy Neptune*. As a result,
the version of Australia which emerges, right from the early
collections, is a complicated one, both as a land to be celebrated
in its original zestful fruitfulness, and as a land haunted by more
disquieting presences and limitations.

In the remainder of this chapter, I will explore the allegiances, themes, and influences which have contributed to Murray's
acts of origination and experiment. The various dispossessions
he has personally felt have contributed to his empathy with the
Aboriginal plight, and to his contentious attempts to translate
their culture – attempts correlative to those of an earlier poetic
movement in Australia, the Jindyworobak – into wider contemporary national consciousness. Those dispossessions have also
intensified his interest in his own family's Gaelic past, whilst
concurrently arousing in him a sense of place and of presence
which seems counter to many of the currents of modernity. And
yet his work displays an adaptability of style and thought not
unaligned to the possibilities to be found elsewhere in modern
writing from Australia and beyond. Discussion of the multiple
relations his writing establishes for itself will form the latter part

of the chapter. Murray's consistent remaking of himself as writer, his taking up and dropping of modes and manners, makes him one of the most exciting of modern writers, yet also one of the best adapted to offer challenging ideas about the direction his country is taking. It is an overview of all of these threads which I seek to provide here.

Les Murray was born into a dairy-farming and forest-working community on the southernmost end of the north coast of New South Wales. His family history, in which his father was denied his natural right to ownership of the family farm after being made to work it unpaid for years by Murray's grandfather, encapsulates many of the issues which were to resonate across his mature poetry, and which were to feed his historical and national vision. Obviously, his father's eventual eviction from the home where Murray was raised, by the cousin who inherited the farm in his place, underpins – in the frequency with which Murray himself returns to it – the anger at injustice (family, social and national) that fuels some of the work he was later to write. Poems like 'Laconics: the Forty Acres' and 'Cowyard Gates', both from the 1977 collection *Ethnic Radio*, reveal deep hurt at the way in which seemingly simple facts of possession of 'our beautiful deep land', as the former poem has it, can become muddled through human blindness and callousness (129). 'Cowyard Gates', which recalls a trip in which Murray drove past his family home after it had been nearly demolished by the cousin, recognizes both the subsequent emotional wounding, and also the complicity which the poet has in the process of destruction itself, not least for the images it furnished for his subsequent rebarbative poetry:

> I had said goodbye to that house many times
> and so helped it fall.
> I have even ransacked it,
> carried off slants of sunlight and of wind
> that used to strike through the bedroom planking, blades
> against the upstart. (156)

These complex feelings of guilt do not, however, overcome those of regret at the destructive action against the former home which he could not have a say in:

> Many feelings are suspended ...
> but, half demolished, it was almost an eddy
> standing there on the ridge,
> memory and loss in a grove of upright boards.

The 'loss' mentioned here has a further particular resonance from the early death of Murray's mother, in what he feels were preventable circumstances. His father, Cecil Murray, subsequently retreated into himself in the house: 'From just on puberty, I lived in funeral: / mother dead of miscarriage, father trying to be dead', as a more recent poem, 'Burning Want' states it (446). And yet that immediate association of 'memory and loss' in 'Cowyard Gates' seems to stand more directly over, and to inform, the tone of much of his other work. This poem in fact appeared in book form after Murray had finally succeeded in resecuring the block of land for his father – as celebrated in 'Laconics' – in 1974 (Murray moved there with his own family in 1986). It also sets the theme for later work which is fascinated with ruined houses, such as 'The Romantic Theme of Ruins' from *The People's Otherworld* (1983), or 'At Min-Min Camp', from the subsequent *The Daylight Moon*, where 'We made camp on a veranda // that had lost its house.' In this latter context, Murray recognizes that such destroyed home environments create in themselves ambiguous responses of both longing and fear, since 'Millions had lived there / on their way to the modern world' (260).

Feelings of disinheritance and dispossession, therefore, also play strongly into Murray's highly complex responses to modernity, which I will return to in their literary and social contexts later in this chapter. More immediately, they established that proximity which Murray has consistently felt between his own experience, in being brought up amongst the rural poor, and that historical brutality enacted upon indigenous Australian people, which I will now explore more fully. This point is made explicitly in the elaborate title of a poem collected in *Lunch and*

Counter Lunch (1974), 'Thinking About Aboriginal Land Rights, I Visit the Farm I Will Not Inherit'. The context of this important poem is that, in the mid-1970s, the Labor government under Gough Whitlam, which had finally won power after decades of conservative rule, adopted the policy that Aborigines were no longer expected, as they had been earlier, to assimilate themselves to white Australia's culture. Aborigines were granted land rights to the Northern Territory in 1974, and a resolution to the effect that the Aborigines and Torres Strait islanders had been 'in prior occupancy of Australia' was passed by the Senate in February 1975, only to be defeated by the House of Representatives.[5] Murray's immediate sense in this poem of this proximity between his own background and that of the Aborigines was to issue most famously in his 'The Buladelah-Taree Holiday Song Cycle', which adapts the form of Aboriginal celebration-poetry, and which was collected in *Ethnic Radio*, and in the essay, also of 1977, 'The Human-Hair Thread'.

As that and other essays make clear, the asserted Aboriginal association goes deeper within his work, and centres once again upon his attitude to local place. In the mid- to late 1980s especially, after his return to live at Bunyah, Murray became fascinated by the spiritual resonance of place, and by the ways in which his own association with places drew together related cultural threads. In an essay first published in 1990, Murray mapped for the reader his own territory:

> The centre of my field of observations is of course my home district of Bunyah, which lies fifty-odd kilometres south of Taree and about twenty kilometres as the crow flies from the Pacific Ocean. In essence, the district comprises the whole upper catchment of the small Wang Wauk river. The Wang Wauk, the name of which meant 'crows' in the local Kattang language, actually behaves more like a real river, or a real crow, and wanders a bit ... The larger region in which I feel and am accepted as native extends from just north of the Manning River down to the top end of the Myall Lakes, and west beyond Gloucester to the foothills of the Dividing Range. (*PT*, 303)

Murray's poems consistently focus upon this territory. But what this mapping essentially establishes is a descriptive consonance between local Aboriginal language and the physical features of the landscape. Territory also acts as a marker of community, acceptance, an assured place from which to make 'observations'. For Murray, particularly at this time, such a sense of territory was related to a 'dimension of dream in art' that he felt ought to be 'especially interesting to Australians', who were becoming increasingly aware of 'terms such as the Dreamtime, dreamings, sacred sites and the like'.

> As I understand it, the categories of the Dreamtime and the sacred are coterminous for the Aborigines. A sacred site is one in which the Dreamtime inheres. The Dreamtime is also a tense, or rather it is all tenses apart from the immediate present and near past ... it is the mythological tense over against the factual, and the place where they meet is the place of ceremony, of art and of law. (*PT*, 346)

Such tenses and a consonant sense of the ceremonial Dreamtime significance of local place had established the curious timelessness of 'The Buladelah-Taree Holiday Song Cycle'. They had also led to the culminating scene of the verse novel, *The Boys Who Stole the Funeral* (1980), where the youthful hero undergoes a hallucinatory initiation and vision of ideal community instructed by Aborigine guides. However anthropologically sound Murray's observations on Dreamtime and sacred sites might be, the question remains as to whether it is ever possible for someone from a settler culture to come to understand fully the relation between ritual performance and place in an indigenous tradition. The ease of translation he makes between the white tradition and the black has itself been cause for concern for some critics. His valorizing adoption of purportedly Aboriginal models for writing in the mid-1970s and early 1980s, sometimes in the *absence* of actual indigenous presences in the poetry, might be seen as part of a troubling trend, identified in white writing by Terry Goldie amongst others, whereby those models are treated as 'historical artefact' rather than as continuing and evolving native resource.[6]

At the time, such attention clearly underpinned a *poetic* consciousness for him, one consonant with certain political exigencies, and one which allowed him to develop a notion of national distinctiveness. It is true to say, however, that, more recently, since the receding of the land-rights issue and the emergence of other national concerns to which he has been equally responsive, Murray has not so earnestly sought to promulgate such a particular sense of the sacred.

However, Murray's fascination with these sacred sites might also be related to his attention to his distinctive European ancestry, descended as he is from a family from Scotland, from the lowland area around the Moray Firth. His concern to trace the Gaelic inheritance had informed what he called the other 'thread', alongside the Aboriginal, in *Ethnic Radio*. In this sense, his feeling for *place* as a bearer of sacred, historical and communal power tunes into the Gaelic tradition of place-name poems (*dindshenchas*), which seek to enact an almost identical resonance. Critics in Australia, though – including some of Murray's earliest and best advocates – have doubted the wisdom of what they see as a special pleading emerging in the poetry around these religious and cultural concerns. The poet and critic Kevin Hart, for instance, sees these issues of cultural recuperation as detrimentally marking work which 'operates increasingly at the level of ideology, not mythology'. He sees such urges as false to the nature of Murray's best writing, writing which proves him as a poet 'more thinking than dreaming or dancing'.[7]

What is clear is that the specific versions of the Aboriginal and Gaelic traditions to which Murray is wedded have had a persistent *poetic* impact within his writing, in both defining its distinctive technique and its formulation of its subjects. In a book review, Murray traced his 'fascination with chiasmus' (the inversion in a second phrase of the order followed in the first) to his reading of translations of Gaelic poetry. His 'continuing passion' for masculine-feminine rhyme derives no doubt from the same communal source (*PT*, 312). In the poem 'The Smell of Coal Smoke', for instance, there are several instances of single syllable words rhyming with two-syllabled ones (day/Café, war/before, chest/starriest). Murray's description of Scots-Australian poetry, and its relation to its native originals, in the essay of 1980 on this part of his inheritance, 'The Bonnie Disproportion', might also stand as a description of his own work. It is also closer to Hart's sense of what his poetry at its truest achieves – 'philosophical concern, mixed with verbal quirkiness, a measure of humour and patches of backward-looking yearning for a light once seen and now extinguished' (*PT*, 123). This truly represents the meditative pace and interest in surprising verbal effects in Murray (as in, perhaps, 'my course is slant' from 'Amanda's Painting' already mentioned), as well as the witty play and memorization caught from the early 'Noonday Axeman' on – 'I will forever ... remember my ancestors, axemen, dairymen, horse-breakers, / now coffined in silence, down with their beards and dreams' (5).

The approach to Aborigine materials, however, seems to have formed something of Murray's style in a larger sense, and relates his work to that of an earlier moment in Australian poetry – the Jindyworobak movement of the late 1930s to the 1950s. In an anthology of Jindyworobak writing in which five of his own poems appeared, Murray is quoted as having claimed half-seriously in a letter to be 'the last of the Jindyworobaks'. The movement was a response, by a group of Adelaide-based poets including Rex Ingamells, Flexmore Hudson, Ian Mudie and Roland Robinson amongst others, to a perceived lack of cultural maturity in the country, a sense that Australia was, as Brian Elliott has written, 'still emotionally and intellectually a colony in adolescence'. In contrast to later writers like A.D. Hope, who sought to establish a continuity with European inheritance, the Jindyworobaks, in seeking to define a national difference, authenticity and uniqueness, turned to Aboriginal culture and ideas. They felt that the poetry of the bush and of the city salon which had predominated in Australia up to that point lacked spirituality, and a true means of describing the relationship between all people and the land they inhabited.

'The Human-Hair Thread' is considered in its statements about the Jindyworobak movement, praising its quest to bring

over the values of the Aboriginal culture and view of the land,
the attempt to fuse Aboriginal and diverse European elements.
But Murray is also alert to the movement's tendency to roman-
ticize the Aborigines themselves, and to the possible racism of
such proclaimed proximities (*PT*, 71). In this, though, the movement's chronicler argues that the original writers were equally
sensitive. Elliott is anxious to point out that their programme was
essentially poetic, that these poets were not seeking to appropriate
and dictate Aboriginal history or morality. The expected audience
for their work was a white one, and the Aboriginal material
figured there as image, symbol and metaphor. Only for Ingamells, the prime manifesto maker of the movement, did the
project carry a more serious cultural force. In his famous piece in
Conditional Culture (1938), which gave the movement its
founding principles, Ingamells pointed out that *jindyworobak*
was an Aboriginal word meaning 'to annex, to join'. 'As he saw
it,' in Elliott's terms, 'the need was to "annex" or "join" the
white to the black, or the black to the white.'[8] Ingamells's
assertion that this founding of a relationship between humanity
and particular lands and climates performed an 'environmental
value', is interpreted by Murray in 'The Human-Hair Thread'
to mean 'a slow moulding of all people within a continent or
region towards the natural human form which that continent or
region demands'. But he accepts that in Australia 'convergence
between black and white is a fact' (*PT*, 96).

Whatever the awkward political implications of such 'fact',
it is clear that 'environmental value' is at the core of Murray's
vision of a distinctive Australian culture and poetics also.[9] From
the early poetry, he celebrated the assimilation of those arriving
in the country to its unique landscapes. As he says in 'The Fire
Autumn', in his second collection, *The Weatherboard Cathedral*
(1969),

> Some who come to our country as being farthest
> out on earth towards the country they sought
> are waiting to hear, where they lie in their deckchairs and
>   graves,
> that, with distance, the serious laws of the universe change,

and more, growing native, still find the limitless country
too near for speech. The dignity growing on trees
in the drystick forests, the mines in the waste land, the
    stones,
are not solar, nor deeply mortal. (35)

Unlike first-generation Australian-born white poets of the
nineteenth century (such as Charles Harpur) who offer founding visions of the relation between settler and the landscape,
Murray is no longer principally preoccupied by the *strangeness*
of the Australian continent, the alienation it sparks in a
European eye. Even in this early poem, Murray describes the
actual European countryside he visits as being 'humanized to
despair', and evokes the 'limitless' qualities of the land into
which the settlers arrive and to which they must adapt. He
continually emphasizes, as the early settlers did, the ancientness
of the land, its new world and primal virtues.

Murray's poetry of place is, therefore, a complex thing.
Sequences like 'The Buladelah-Taree Holiday Song Cycle' show
him, however, contentiously deploying an Aboriginal form in
order to establish his own modern, Gaelic settler view of the
landscape's sacred places. Another sequence, 'The Idyll Wheel',
which was written soon after Murray's return to live on the
family's forty acres at Bunyah in the mid-1980s, joins early
work like 'Evening Alone at Bunyah' from *The Weatherboard
Cathedral* in suggesting that the primary sacred place for the
poet is that of his family farm. And yet, as the holiday song cycle
also suggests, Murray is attuned to the perspectives of
journeying, the sense that the country is to be passed through
and arrived at as well as lived within ('It is good to come out
after driving and walk on bare grass / relearning that country')
(139). As his poetry might seem sometimes to render a Hesiod-
like rhythm of works and days, it therefore *also* has a more
Homeric inflection, one which is attuned to the demands, ancient,
modern, and also traditional in Australia, of being on the road,
of droving, journeying, and wandering.

Once again, Murray bears, in this, a complex and revision-
ary relationship with one of the most famous of his seemingly

absolute, as stated, positions. One of the most significant disputes with which Murray became involved was a wrangle at the end of the 1970s with the expatriate Australian poet Peter Porter, which it is worthwhile looking at more closely. In his essay 'On Sitting Back and Thinking About Porter's Boeotia', he provides a critical commentary on his friend's poem 'On First Looking Into Chapman's Hesiod'. What he discovers there is that the rural crafts tradition within the Greek pastoral landscape of Boeotia, celebrated by Hesiod via Chapman, is actually being relegated by Porter himself. Porter, in other words, seems in this poem to be following a tradition whereby Boeotia is rendered almost comic from the perspective of the capital city, Athens, place of progressiveness and classic, intellectual art (Porter's poem includes the lines 'I still seek / The permanently upright city where / Speech is nature and plants conceive in pots').[10] Athens is also, of course, the site of a cultural inheritance which, through imperial conquest, was imposed upon other native and national traditions.

Murray feels that, for Porter, Boeotia provides a model for the backward-lookingness of rural Australian life, one which, despite the Athenian models which are available to it, is a model that Australian art has neither appropriated nor successfully thrown off in developing its modern national aesthetic. To a certain extent, Murray clearly agrees with Porter's view, finding the culture 'colonially obedient', and arguing that 'any distinctiveness we possess *is* still firmly anchored in the bush', the rural heartland of the nation (*PT*, 61). But, what he clearly also resents in Porter's view is the sense that the bush is the place of the *hoi polloi*, the uneducated ockers unable to match the achievements of the city elite. Rather, he sees in that Boeotian-ness a resource which might outlast 'the period of collapse of many of our parent cultures', and also something which is a 'resource of immeasurable value to us all' through the culture of the nation's original Boeotians, the black Australians, as he calls them (64).

As such, Murray concludes, Australia might have, against the clichéd attitude reflected by Porter, a unique opportunity to establish an original model of national society, 'the long-needed reconciliation of Athens with Boeotia, and create that lasting organic country where *urban* and *rural* no longer imply a conflict'. Once again, therefore, we find Murray positing a surprisingly conciliatory, though idealistic, possibility. Where his own sense of the sacredness of place, which in the essay he relates to the Boeotian outlook, and not the Athenian, would seem to imply that his own view is strictly *opposed* to Porter's, in fact he seeks a flexibility between the two views. Whilst a work like 'Sydney and the Bush' from *Ethnic Radio* had seemed to suggest that 'there is no common ground' between the two (124), the sequence 'The Sydney Highrise Variations' from *The People's Otherworld* (1983), sees him relishing, if ambiguously, the prospects opened by such things as the new Gladesville Road Bridge: 'It feels good. It feels right. / The joy of sitting high is in our judgement. / The marvellous brute-force effects our century work' (172).[11] Brute force is associated also, of course, with Nazis and Stalinists, but the exhilaration and literal exorbitance of the celebration are nonetheless palpable ('it's a space-probe, / a trajectory of strange fixed dusts').

This sense, not of ambivalence towards the properties and contexts of the modern world, but of the *multivalence* to be found there, and of the polyvalent traditions open to the modern writer, emerged once the Boeotian and Athenian debate was resurrected in the pages of the newly formed magazine *Kunapipi* in 1979. In response to a hostile review of *Ethnic Radio* by Mark O'Connor, which equated the Boeotian in Murray with a reactionary politics, the poet replied that 'I'm not really a social conservative … What I really am is a historicist or cultural relativist, in the sense that I bear it in mind that there have been and will be other times, and other opinions than those prevailing at the moment.' Murray therefore eschews the 'loose terms open to rhetorical abuse', such as 'Conservative, Progressive, Radical and the like', as alien to 'my thinking'.[12] Once again, we find Murray in this response refusing labels, refusing to stand still. The dismissal of 'loose terms' establishes the poet's duty towards the language as against the critic's. As we will frequently see in this book, Murray's claim to be alert to the relative nature of 'opinion' establishes both the dramatic provocation of his own intervention into quotidian cultural and political debate, and the implicitly critical stance of the poetry itself. Whilst he might *seem* to be taking a stance which is against the metropolitan superficiality of modernity, he is saying that in truth he does so for a purpose, the purpose of unsettling complacency and of revealing verbal delusion. He does not deny that such is the condition of modernity, however uneasy he might feel about it. Yet he also celebrates those aspects of technology and speed which appeal to him.

More practically, Murray's experience as a travelling poet finds its way into various of his works, in nearly all collections from early on. Early works of empathy with home-comers, like 'Troop Train Returning', find equal but opposite delighted expressions in poems such as 'The Away-Bound Train', and 'Vindaloo in Merthyr Tydfil'. We are reminded by Murray that he is a wearied traveller and reader on the international poetry circuit in nearly every collection from the early 1970s, when he gave up translation work in order to write full-time. Poems like 'The Cardiff Commonwealth Arts Festival Poetry Conference 1965, Recalled', 'The International Poetry Festivals Thing' and 'The International Terminal' show a scepticism about the whole process of, and the demands on, a modern poet's life. But they are extensions of a similar but more local impulse to be found amongst many other poems. The title 'Portrait of the Autist as a New World Driver', from *Lunch and Counter Lunch* (1974), reveals both Murray's dogged and wily adherence to a version of himself as a self-absorbed, uneducated, deeply conservative resister of everything in the modern environment, and his role as a mobile, literary enacter of a new modern possibility. The culmination of such portraits of on-the-road 'autism' in Murray's work is the title-character of the long verse novel and folk-epic, *Fredy Neptune* (1998). Fred moves from his local situation 'on our farm just outside Dungog' to witness many of the atrocities in the first half of the twentieth century, as he constantly moves on across Europe and the United States. Often not in control of his future direction, and with a superhuman strength gained from a bodily insensateness due to his presence at a massacre of women in Armenia, Fred's story is a modern *Odyssey* which counters the more allusive renditions of Homer by the modernists themselves, including Pound and Joyce.

Of course, this sense of journeying across country and between country and city has its basis in Murray's cultural and personal concerns. It reflects the nomadism of Aboriginal culture, the movement between sacred places. Murray's travels between Australia and Europe, and his poetic reflections on the histories and landscapes encountered, reverse the emigration of his ancestors and of many other Australians in the middle of the nineteenth century. The displacements and unsettlements involved reflect also that family history which I described above, but also Murray's own leaving of Bunyah for an education at Sydney University in the late 1950s, a time of his life celebrated in the 'spiral of sonnets' gathered in *Lunch and Counter Lunch*, and called after the university's motto, 'Sidere Mens Eadem Mutato'. Murray also had several years living as a hobo during his prolonged studies for a degree, years during which he wandered the Australian interior, as poems like 'Recourse to the Wilderness' relate.

More specifically, as spatial and geographical Australian historians have been concerned to suggest, journeying was crucial to the establishment of a sense of what Australia is. The early voyages of exploration into the interior by men such as Eyre, Leichhardt, Sturt, Mitchell and Stuart formed legendary models of heroism against hostile conditions and climate which have obtained a place at the centre of the national imagination, informing, perhaps most famously, Patrick White's novel *Voss*. As Sue Rowley has asserted in an essay on 'Australian Bush Mythology', 'the centrality of the journey theme as a metaphoric and structural device in national imagery and narrative is not purely the function of historical mobility. Journeying infuses the representation of explorers, pioneers and bushmen with the potency of quest, the pilgrimage and the passage of life itself.'[13] Murray essentially translates the cattle-drover's or bush journeyman's perspective of his ancestors into the context of modern life.

But he again retains an ambiguous and complex sense of the *distinctiveness* of that perspective. Rowley pertinently quotes a sentence from the most famous story, 'The Drover's Wife', by Henry Lawson, one of the pioneering fictional writers about bush culture: 'You might walk for twenty miles along this track without being able to fix a point in your mind, unless you are a bushman.' This contains both a sense of the familiarity with the land which excludes the outsider, and a sense that the bush lacks a perspective familiar to the European; the sense that by 'fixing a point' it is possible to establish visual depth in the landscape, a depth which might then stand in for a more reflective mental perspective. In a poem by Murray like 'Aspects of Language and War on the Gloucester Road', it is clear that he can fix those points, points of personal familiarity and local history which would be passed over by an outsider, and this is what forms the substance and the communal ambition of the poem: for example, 'There's a house where I had hospitality / without fuss for years when I needed it' (281).

Yet, as the title and impetus of a poem from *Dog Fox Field* (1990) confirms, Murray's version of Australia includes that other perspective of the land gained by travelling beyond the familiar home district. 'The Assimilation of Background' ends with a vision that 'on that bare, crusted country / background and foreground had merged' (337), a vision repeated in the ideal mental landscape of 'Equanimity', 'Where nothing is diminished by perspective' (181). As a result, the poetry shares outlandishly with perspectives of 'God's common immortality', as an earlier poem from *The People's Otherworld* discovers in the emu, an image of 'daylight detail, aggregate, in process' (204). The lack of foreground and background in the interior means that there are no fixed points, but rather an accumulation of details gathered along the way. As a result, Murray's writing attunes itself to the Australian perspective, in acting at an intersection of the temporal with the spatial. Movement onwards through time in the interior is the only way of gauging the crossing of space.

Australian consciousness, therefore, shares in 'The Quality of Sprawl', as Murray famously named it in another poem from that collection – a resistance to limitation and to hierarchical perceptions of space and thence of value, which hold sway in the old world.

Paul Carter has argued, through study of the diary narratives of their journeys provided by the original explorers of the interior, that 'despite the linear appearance of the text', their writing is 'characterized by a non-linear narration of events. The sequence of sentences belies the discontinuity of the content – the fact that the country is constantly open to baffling change, surprising reversals ... verb tenses oscillate uncertainly between past and present.'[14] From early to late, Murray's work itself has been characterized by such 'surprising reversals' and switches of direction, particularly at the end of poems. The second poem in the *Collected Poems*, for instance, describes a 'Tableau in January', a noon in the Australian summer in which the sun's radiance (in contrast to Yeats's modernist apocalyptic view of European history) makes 'things drift apart'. Yet the final lines of the poem bring us a return to the figure of the poem's speaker, the poet himself 'smiling' where 'there is more light than world', who 'Takes his soft lines and bends them where they meet' (2). This is an important early instance of the role consistently given to the poem itself in Murray's national vision as a centring and focusing of the climate and space, which otherwise elude articulation. For him, poetry, in other words, stands in for that 'Australia, part imaginary and part historical' which is repressed within colonialism, but which forms the centre of the emergent 'Republic', as he sees it (*PT*, 46).

Even so, the work continues to be *stylistically* characterized by those traits which Carter associates with the particular early journeying across the continent itself: the associations of locale and language. 'The Holy Show', from *Conscious and Verbal*, movingly recalls the class prejudice which operated in Murray's childhood neighbourhood. Having been dressed in his best to attend a Christmas party, the child-poet is remembered being beaten and grabbed by children from richer families 'in the great

shame of our poverty', and for thinking Christmas 'undivided, /
whereas it's all owned'. The final lines turn back upon the
remembered woe of Murray's parents at the incident:

> Once away, they angrily softened to
> me squalling, because I was their kiddie
> and had been right about the holy show
> that models how the world should be
> and could be, shared, glittering in near focus
>
> right out to the Sex frontier. (74)

This displays vernacular usage ('Once away … I was their
kiddie'), which acts as a distinguishing device in itself by setting
the poem apart from 'standard' English. The rhythm of the voice
and syntax, which runs against and across the pentameters ('right
about the holy show / that models how'), also tunes into a local
idiom, although the 'standard' model remains vestigially present
throughout.[15] The complex assonance and sound-patterning of
this writing (as, for example, in 'shared … near … frontier')
offer what Murray has come to think of as a kind of jazz made
upon traditional metre and rhyme, providing a distinctive
musical structuring to his deployment of the vernacular in
poetry that is present in all examples quoted in this book. Here
in this complex sequence of tense switches, the child's vision of
social justice is mapped onto a radiant vision of possibility from
which it is not possible to stand back and make a different
judgement. Yet, in the surprising and literally detached final
line, we find Murray strikingly eliding two kinds of shame –
that brought upon by unlooked-for affirmations of family poverty,
such as that which forms the central story of the poem, and that
sexual shaming which, as he has narrated several times, haunted
him from the time of childhood playground incidents.

As an overweight child, himself prone to 'sprawl', Murray
was subjected to cruel taunts by the girls amongst his peers. This
partly created in him, he says in a memoir, 'a buried fury of sex
and a terror of women'.[16] Without exculpating him, that fury and
terror clearly have a role in the misogyny and anti-feminism of
some of Murray's writing, particularly in the verse novel *The*

Boys Who Stole the Funeral (1980), which ends with a militant feminist being maimed for life with boiling water. They also generate his troubled relationship to iconic national models of identity founded upon masculinity, an effect that I will discuss many times in this book.[17] Kay Schaffer has noted that, from the outset of bush nationalism, male writers in Australia reinforced gender divisions with difficulty: 'The bush threatens to reduce men to exhibiting characteristics which Western culture assumes are feminine … passivity, weakness, depression, despair.' As a result, Schaffer sees men there resorting to a version of male bonding, mateship, which is clearly vital to Murray also.[18] Women are often invisible in Murray's writing, and, as will become clear below, he sees the feminist movement as largely American in origin, and therefore alien to Australian life. And yet, in the poems to his wife Valerie, and in the epithalamiums which form key generic and unitary markers in his work, there is a strength perceived within a balanced relation between the sexes.

Yet, in the painful 'The Holy Show', we find that rapid elision of seemingly discontinuous content which Carter feels to be the founding distinctiveness of Australian writing. That rapid elision had, of course, characterized something of the class and cultural 'alliances' contentiously perceived by Murray which I have been discussing throughout this opening chapter. These form, for instance, his sense of the poetic potential shared by Jindyworobak and Aboriginal poetry, and also by Gaelic work. It is an elision which lies both at the heart of his vision of an ideal Australia, an 'inclusive Creole Australia' as he has put it, and that 'anti-discrimination' in his thinking which he feels is opposed by various interest groups in both the literary world and the elite political caste.[19] In fact, what we might see as Murray's controversial translation of the concept of 'Creole', which originated from the polydialectical base of other colonial contact zones (including West Africa, the Caribbean, South America and Mauritius), into his local context might also be taken to achieve these things. As Ashcroft, Griffiths and Tiffin have argued, the 'Creole linguistic continuum in English' proves that 'the language is constituted of several overlapping lects or distinguishable forms of language use', and 'affirms the plurality of practice in any one geographical space'. Yet, and this is a further implication favourable to Murray beyond the internal national cultural and political one, in this overturning of 'concentric' notions of language which regard 'standard' English as a 'core', these three critics see Creole as offering 'a paradigmatic demonstration of the abrogating impetus in post-colonial theory (and presumably literature). Creole refuses the categories of imperial culture.'[20]

It was in essays such as 'The Australian Republic' (1976), written in response to the dismissal of Gough Whitlam's Labor government by the Governor-General Sir John Kerr on 11 November 1975, that Murray first emerged as a prominent propagandist for the republican ideal (his protest goes along with similar outcries from other writers, including, perhaps most prominently, Patrick White). There, given the nature of the response to this dismissal, Murray concentrates his attacks on the colonial situation, which forces, he says, 'the vernacular culture' to retreat 'into rituals and semi-autistic meditation' (50). Yet he also expresses his unease with the arrival of an indigenous 'educated caste', which he sees as gradually replacing the colonial Establishment in the country, a new ascendancy which 'is the natural upper class of a socialist world order' (PT, 48). Whitlam had himself, unlike the conservative forces of government which preceded him, concentrated on alleviating the needs and frustrations of the new working class in Australia's big cities. He 'often behaved,' as the historian Geoffrey Bolton has put it, 'as if the sun rose over Sydney and set over Canberra'.[21] In other words, he never took the rest of Australia very seriously. Murray, with his strong feeling that the heart of republican distinctiveness lay close to his own rural origins, must also have been attacking, in his charges against the newly educated class, the shift in the focus of power away from the poor in the 1970s, from the people he grew up among. However, 'The Australian Republic' ends by celebrating the fact that the Whitlam years had at least seen the emergence in politics of the ideals of *equality* and *fraternity*, and takes heart from the fact that, once the value of these ideals had been perceived, the republic could not be far off.

These ideals were to be restated at a later stage of the republican debate, in the light of the controversy which Murray entered, having been asked in 1998 to collaborate with Prime Minister John Howard in drafting a putative preamble to the constitution of the country. 'The Preamble's Bottom Line', as it stands in the most recent version, in the essay of that title, reads as follows: 'Australia's democratic federal system of government exists under law to preserve each person in an equal dignity which may never be infringed by prejudice or fashion or ideology, nor invoked against merit.' Beyond the equity of this, though, as the essay reveals, are a number of attempts to resist what Murray perceives as 'the coercive use of items on the current political agenda', including what he feels is the excessive amount of guilt felt by the white liberal conscience in respect of their ancestors' treatment of the Aborigines.

Murray's view of this is very Joycean, echoing at some distance Leopold Bloom's assertion of his nationality in the face of a reductive and outmoded version from the nationalist bar-room Citizen in *Ulysses*. 'I was born here', Murray, like Bloom, records, 'and have lived my life here; under Aboriginal law I have as much right to country as they. The British government stole our continent two hundred years ago.'[22] This passage shares the strange temporality, and seemingly odd sense of the possessive, of much of Murray's poetry, as well as the rapid shifts of subject matter and perspective. Whatever the (obviously angry and intense) sense of personal victimization and isolation which Murray feels that he has suffered because of his views (and he notes again here the newspaper charge of racism made against him), it is clear that his vision of a creolized republic is entirely consistent with his vision of the destruction of hierarchies inherent in any relationship with the Australian landscape, whether the black's or the white's. Contrary to what might seem a reactionary tendency in Murray's resistance to current liberal thought on race and other issues, 'The Preamble's Bottom Line'

again celebrates what Murray sees as old Left or Labor
achievements in Australia, including the introduction of the
secret ballot, which was essential to the liberation of the people
not only here but elsewhere.

This countering strain of thought had taken Murray into
unpopular territory before. In an essay on 'Eric Rolls and the
Golden Disobedience' (1982), he had admitted his debt to books
such as Russel Ward's *Australian Legend* and J.S. Manifold's
Who Wrote the Ballads. Manifold argues that the non-convict
English administrators and free settlers had little to do with the
founding of 'an Australian culture or an Australian nationhood'.
Moreover, it was the convicts and the Australian-born whites,
often uneducated, who could 'create a language, verbal and
musical' which was true to the identity of the country. Because
of this illiteracy, the manifestations of this culture were captured
through ballads, many of which celebrated bushrangers such as
Hall, McGuire and Ned Kelly, who had preyed upon rich
farmers, and had eluded the police by retreating into the bush.[23]
Murray was clearly influenced early on by the most famous of
the balladeers, Banjo Paterson, and has himself adopted variants
of the ballad form in poems including 'The Ballad Trap', 'The
Ballad of Jimmy Governor', 'Inverse Ballad', and 'The Ballad of
the Barbed Wire Ocean', down to 'The Relative Gold' from
Conscious and Verbal. The culture that such works celebrate,
however precariously (for, as the early 'The Ballad Trap'
acknowledges, 'The ballad ends with … death' (32)), clearly
underpins that version of the '"folk" Australia' that essays like
'The Australian Republic' claim to be 'the real matrix of any
distinctiveness we possess as a nation'. They form that 'vernacular republic' towards which all of Murray's poetry is aimed,
and which famously formed the title of his most popular book in
Australia, his first volume of selected poems (*PT*, 46).

More recent critics in the country have, of course, challenged
the narrowness and limitation of the romanticized version of
bush nationalism put forward by such authors as Ward and
Manifold. G.A. Wilkes has pointed out that, in fact, the
purported democracy of the bush life was underpinned by a

continuing set of class and gender hierarchies. He has argued in contrast for the valuable contribution to a distinctive version of Australian-ness from the culture of the big cities, and has seen the continuing cosmopolitanism provided by the historical links with Europe as being crucial to the nation's future.[24] Yet, as I have argued, Murray's version of this nationalism is in itself a complex and multifaceted idea, 'part imaginary and part historical' (PT, 38). To that extent, it establishes itself close to that space which Benedict Anderson has famously called an 'imagined community', one conforming to no single reality, but inventing a self-image to resist the history of colonization in his country.[25] Whatever the value for him of the Ward and Manifold vision, even the titles of his own 'ballads' suggest his unease with simply accepting it as a given. The sheer multiplicity of his work offers, as I have been saying, a version of what in one review, the year before the republican essay, he called that 'Homeric many-mindedness and sense of wrestling with complexities of sense and music that has been the spinal strength of Western poetry' (PT, 33).

There are, inevitably, tonal as well as cultural and political implications within such diversity. Even when treating of his centring subjects, Murray has recognized that the specific version of the Homeric open to Australian writers allows for a greater tonal freedom than was perhaps available elsewhere. In an early review of the English poet Jon Silkin, for example, he argued that poets alert to working-class history in Britain 'have come to regard grace, wit, gaiety, and delight as culpable connivance with privilege ... concentration on suffering to the exclusion of much else that is true is a European mood, and mode, which may be passing ... In the New World, happiness is permitted.'[26] Elsewhere, he has claimed that 'the ability to laugh at venerated things ... a spiritual laughter' may, in time, 'prove to be one of Australia's great gifts to mankind' (PT, 147). That laughter gives a brio to a great many of his images, and smacks back at Europe. As when, in 'Shower', he has made us delight in 'this enveloping passion of Australians', he concludes the poem in a deadpan way by naughtily reminding us that 'Only in England is its name an unkind word; / only in Europe is it enjoyed by telephone' (183). These swift humorous changes of direction and rabbit punches will be returned to often in what follows.

Such tonal switches and many-mindedness inevitably make any discussion of Murray's intertexts a complex issue, as the combination of the Jindyworobak and the Gaelic in his work outlined above suggests. Partly, as Murray himself has argued, this complexity derives from the nature of the colonial condition in which he has operated. As he told Lawrence Bourke, when thinking about the notion of an Australian literary tradition, 'There's a flavour, there's a feel, there's a tone, but I'm not sure about a tradition. You can probably distinguish several, and none of them is complete, or stands on its own.'[27] A large part of Murray's own extra-poetic activity, beside his forays into the politics of the moment, has been concerned, partly as a result of this sense of there being several strands to tradition, with establishing what is distinctive, and therefore useful, in prior literature. The commitment to multiplicity (together with the core feeling that poetry must respect the 'vernacular' energies in the country), has meant that Murray's work, although often difficult in the kinds of 'complexities of sense' with which it engages, is rarely directly allusive – as much modern poetry, in the wake of early twentieth-century practice, has become.

A rare instance of such reference in Murray's work is paradoxically provided by the sonnet which stood at the opening of the 1974 collection, *Lunch and Counter Lunch*. It was originally called 'Dedication, Written Last: For the Vernacular Republic', but has been subsequently retitled as 'The Mitchells'. A swagman, Jack Mitchell, had appeared as the central figure in some of the republican Henry Lawson's stories 'Mitchell: A Character Sketch' and 'On the Edge of a Plain'. Lawson (1867–1922), notoriously, only left Sydney briefly to visit Bourke and Hungerford in the bush, but the spoken energy of his short stories for the city's republican magazine, the *Bulletin*, clearly provide one model for Murray's own sense of the 'vernacular'. Lawson's view of 'the grand Australian bush', as given for instance at the end of 'The Bush Undertaker', stands behind the lonely and isolated characters who people particularly Murray's earlier collections, like the figure in the poem 'The Widower in the Country'. The bush, for Lawson, is 'the tutor of eccentric minds, the home of the weird, and of much that is different from things in other lands.'[28] On the other hand, and in contrast again, Murray's vision of 'the bush, or as we now say the Land' in a poem like 'Louvres', as 'the three quarters of our continent / set aside for mystic poetry', also taps both the 'environmental values' of the Jindyworobaks, and that visionary quality of the interior given expression even by the visiting D.H. Lawrence in his novel *Kangaroo* (241).

Despite the Lawson-like 'folk' elements, in other words, Murray's writing remains difficult, with a density which demands patience from its readers, and a certain amount of study of its tone and idiom. At the level of the writing's subject-matter, this obliquity can sometimes be put down to the autodidacticism which Murray has frequently advertized as central to his thinking, despite his university degree. 'As a small boy he read [his mother's school] prize books', Helen Frizell wrote in an interview-article, and 'went right through a set of Cassell's Encyclopaedia ("It gave me an interest in everything. I've always wanted to write about everything.")'.[29] Later, as a university student in Sydney, he ignored the course reading lists, and read the Fisher library instead in 'a plan-free mass querying / of condensed humans off the shelves' (*CV*, 34). Such an oblique take upon learning might be also put down to what, in 'The Shield-Scales of Heraldry', which employs a typically abstruse but apposite vocabulary, he calls his life as 'a half-autistic // kid in scrub paddocks vert'. This is a state which he also attributes to the colonial status of his country, locked in (as quoted above) 'semi-autistic meditation' (439). Murray's complex sense of the multi-threadedness of his cultural position always goes along, therefore, with a personal interest in vocabularies and perspectives which abut on the everyday, but which also counter it, and concurrently inject new life into the idioms of the poetry.

Murray's feeling for the need to establish a place amidst the several strands of Australian tradition has led most obviously to his editorship of three anthologies of Australian poetry. In his *New Oxford Book of Australian Verse* (1986), what we find most noteworthy is an attempt to rediscover the 'varied, idiosyncratic' poetic scene which existed in Australia prior to Lawson's attacks on literary gentility, a scene which has, Murray thinks, largely become obscured by those attacks. In the essay reflecting on the experience of gathering the materials for the anthology, Murray praises 'The Narrow-Columned Middle Ground' of nineteenth-century Australian poetry, which mostly appeared anonymously in the newspapers of the day. This was a poetry which, unlike more literary contemporary versions, accepted the Australian environment totally, and as a result adopted a 'middle style', open – as Murray's own work is – to the distinctive oral energies of the country but also to the civil qualities of written verse (*PT*, 225). The 'middle style', in other words, when translated into a contemporary context, might offer a model for his introduction into the space of the poem of the distinctive vernacular energies of the nation. This is that model which, from at least the time of the essay on 'The Australian Republic', had seemed to suggest that the poem might 'stand in' for the ideal shape which such a republic might take. It is also a further reflection of that 'double aspect' which Wright identifies in all Australian poetry.

To explore this a little further, throughout Murray's work there has been a suggestion, analogous to that made by the English poet W.H. Auden, that the form of the poem might offer an ideal of social and civic possibility yet to be enacted by the mechanisms of the state itself. That 'wilful confusion of parts of speech, as well as a deliberately recherché vocabulary' which, in an early review, Murray celebrated in Auden's last book clearly provides a further model for his own writing (28). Following his quest for a national poetic style, his writing displays something of 'Auden's dancing seriousness', his 'absolute mastery of airy, civilized verse', and shows him to be a 'great partaker in the intellectual conversation of mankind' (Auden also being interested throughout his career in the use of abstruse and technical words) (*PT*, 27).[30] In a sequence like 'The Sunraysia

Poems' from *Conscious and Verbal*, we find Murray revisiting the values of friendship within a particular landscape and domestic space, in ways that strongly suggest the continuing possibilities he discovers in Auden. Recalling a drive taken with an unnamed companion, 'we mentioned again / unsecured farm doors, open / verandahs, /separate houses, / emblems of a good society' (54). The retrospective nature of this reported conversation, celebrating a possibility which modern Australia has ignored, is to the point. 'I go my way, looking back sometimes, looking around me', as 'The Gum Forest' has it (151).

The civic model offered by the poems can be a lost possibility, as well as an aspiration, as seen from the vantage point of the present. Such retrospectives set Murray's work apart from that of the most prominent of other contemporary Australian poets sharing a combination of desire to tap the nation's colloquial energies in his writing and political instinct (a very different one from Murray's), Bruce Dawe. The setting of Dawe's work amidst the city suburbs, which he feels represent the true situation of modern humanity, is at odds with the other, familial and rural, energies which Murray is concerned to listen to and harness in his poems.

Underlying the drive towards founding a separate Australian poetics upon the spoken idioms of the country, therefore, there consistently lies in Murray an ear for 'civil qualities'. Even as his writing distinctively sprawls across the page, those features of poetic space allow it to offer a model for a better social possibility than that actually existing. Murray's ideal '"folk" Australia', the basis for a hoped-for vernacular republic, remains 'part imaginary, part historical', and on both sides of the equation the poet finds a part to play in realizing that republic, not least by putting into circulation those aspects of the country's literary tradition which he feels have been neglected or wilfully overlooked by the literary and academic establishment.[31] The recovery of verse from newspapers of the nineteenth century rests alongside his many other national and international literary interests, to form part of the quest for a separate intertextuality and Australian literary tradition where he feels that none exists.

Intertextuality in Murray is, therefore, despite his anthologizing interests, a complex *process*. It is elusive in its determined effort to make a tradition from what there is, as the necessary condition of that colonial inheritance within which Murray found himself. Like the shape of 'The Pole Barns' of which he writes in *Dog Fox Field*, 'each line' of Murray's own poetry 'ends in memorial axemanship' (317).

Within twentieth-century Australian poetry, there can be no doubt that the primary model of those 'civil qualities' for Murray, and the primary influence on all of his writing, is that of Kenneth Slessor. In another of his anthologies, *Fivefathers: Five Australian Poets of the Pre-Academic era*, a presentation of the work of hard-to-obtain key Australian male poets for the British market, Murray sets Slessor at the head, albeit slightly disingenuously: 'Many consider Slessor the greatest of all Australian poets.' The question of Slessor's significance for Murray, and of his influence upon the later poet, is again a difficult one. Slessor, as Murray's brief preface to his selection from his work notes, was 'adamantly opposed in his maturity to the older Australian ballad tradition', and hence dismissive of the very vernacular energies Murray is, even if awkwardly, tuned in to. Slessor, as an emergent writer in what he himself saw as the first period of his work, 1919–26, was part of the group gathered around the visionary artist and writer Norman Lindsay. Lindsay rejected the native tradition in favour of a mishmash of European Romantic and Symbolist influences, favouring personal discovery and sexual and moral experiment over what he saw as the cloying parochialism of Australian life. The ornate surface of Slessor's early work shows the impact of this preciousness: a typical line from an early poem included by Murray here running 'I saw the bottomless, black cups of space.'[32]

More seemingly unsettling from Murray's perspective is Slessor's assimilation in his work from 1927 onwards of the influence of T.S. Eliot in particular, but also of Ezra Pound, the subject of a hostile early review by Murray, 'Pound Devalued'. There, Murray has no hesitation in charging Pound and Eliot with delivering poetry over to the self-consciously intellectual elite which was contemporaneously emerging in universities, and in establishing a 'slangy-mandarin' tone which subsequent writing has never escaped from (*PT*, 16).[33] Slessor's fascination seems more complex though, related as it is to the Romantic/Symbolist inheritance imbibed from Lindsay. He seems to have found in Eliot's cityscapes a tone which could be adapted to his own wearied sense of defiantly disillusioned life in modern Sydney. In 'William Street', for instance, another poem included by Murray in his selection, Slessor reviews the sensory qualities of the city and relishes them against possible dissent: 'Smells rich and rasping, smoke and fat and fish.' As the mock-aggressive refrain at the end of each of the four verses runs, 'You find this ugly, I find it lovely.'[34] More particularly, Slessor's Eliotic preoccupation with time, its erosions and moments of transcendence, as evidenced in sequences like 'Out of Time' and his stirringly beautiful elegy 'Five Bells', finds its own echoes in Murray. It comes through both in his interest in Aboriginal Dreamtime, and also in the signals sent by titles such as 'The Future' and 'The Past Ever Present'. Sequences like 'Walking to the Cattle Place' seem, in both implication and manner, to want to still time itself, as, at the end of a meditatory twenty-two pages, we are told 'I have travelled one day' (77). 'In the silent lands / time broadens into space', as lines from *The Weatherboard Cathedral* have it (26). That kind of category disruption marks Murray's distance from the divisions of European consciousness.

Yet, as his deployment of such traditional features as the refrain suggests, Slessor held on, despite his excitement at, and empathy with, the European modernist perspective, to a conservative poetic style, as Murray has himself done, whilst also adopting a freer style, but still a measured one, as occasion demanded. Slessor's resulting controlled urbanity is not quite Murray's note, but yet it offers a further version of that 'middle style', half way between the colloquial and the refinements of the literary canon, which Murray is also after. As Andrew Taylor has suggested, Slessor ultimately fully adopted none of the influences with which he dallied at various points in his career, and the same could be said of Murray. Yet, with Murray as with Slessor, in Taylor's words on this issue of influences, 'it was nonetheless the relentless demands he made on them that forced them to reveal their inadequacies and made him displace them, eventually replacing them with nothing but the energy of his own imagination.' This, Taylor concludes, casts Slessor in 'the true role of the modernist who can expect meaning, order, significance neither from nature ... ("South Country"), nor from society ... ("Last Trams")'.[35]

In a section from the sequence 'The Atlas' (included in *Fivefathers*), Slessor celebrates 'the world no tide may stir' which a 'great cartographer' has managed to create in mapping the Dutch seacoast. Yet, in reaction, Slessor feels jealousy at such timeless stilled perfectionism, and the section ends with a typical piece of Romantic afflatus:

> O, could he but clap up like this
> My decomposed metropolis,
> Those other countries of the mind,
> So tousled, dark and undefined![36]

Murray's adherence to a vernacular style would resist such grandiose claims, particularly the theatrical suggestion of a further, darker unconscious, which both reflects but also supersedes the condition of the modern city. And yet, at the same time, he would accept the Romantic notion that the mind projects its own, partly experiential, and partly idealized, realities. 'This country is my mind,' as the early sequence 'Evening Alone at Bunyah' has it; 'I lift my face / and count my hills' (15). Murray's Australia self-proclaimedly emerges from his own conception of it, in other words. In this, he reflects the distinctiveness and self-constriction of the conditions of enquiry which Paul Carter again has traced in the early colonists of the country.

The white 'founders' did not set out, Carter claims, to establish a colony which is Australia. Rather, they consistently adopted and adapted themselves to the conditions which they came upon in their travels over the new lands, and in their recordings of those travels. This sense of the country as a partly imaginative product, Carter urges, meant that 'the new country was a rhetorical construction, a product of language and the intentional gaze, not of the detached, dictionary-clasping spectator.' As a result of this, and of the particular unimpeded vagrancy of the imagination offered by the vast space of the interior, the English language was itself forced to adapt to local conditions, since, as Carter suggests, 'there seemed to be nothing that could be accurately named.'[37]

This sense that the work of naming is still ongoing in Australia underpins Murray's own fascination with words and with names, more especially what he calls, in the title of a section of the sequence 'Walking to the Cattle Place', 'The Names of the Humble', those hitherto relegated within world literature. It underpins also his Slessor-like unease with any one mode of writing, an unease which, when taken with his Romantic perspective, fuelled his famous and ongoing dispute with the younger writers emerging in Australia in the early 1970s. Anthologies of the time with a polemical bent, including Thomas W. Shapcott's *Australian Poetry Now* and Alexander Craig's *12 Poets 1950–1970*, lamented the traditionalism of Australian poetry, and its resistance to the kinds of formal experiment being promulgated by postmodern American poets. Shapcott celebrates the possibilities for 'zeal and recklessness' within the work of this new generation who, unlike their immediate predecessors, escaped growing up 'literally in the shadow of the War and the Bomb'.[38]

Murray's work appeared in both anthologies, but rested uneasily alongside their pro-American ethos. His introductory statement to the selection of his work in Shapcott's volume seems almost deliberately poised to stand against such influence, insisting instead that 'my poems have a certain first-person continuity to them, a speaking character who is variously myself and who ebbs and flows in the degree of his overt involvement with themes.'[39] That sense of the continuity of the first person in his writing has mounted his challenge to the American-influenced poetry which was just about to appear from writers such as John Tranter and Robert Adamson, writers influenced by the Black Mountain and New York School ethos of Donald Hall's seminal anthology of 1960, *The New American Poetry*. This is a decentred poetry of the new Left radicalism and drug culture which emerged from the 1960s, a poetry deeply sceptical of the retention of that very first-person voice to which Murray has held, and of the formal traditionalism which frequently accompanies it. Much of the political energy for this writing derived from the Australian protests against the Vietnam War, protests which took the same form as those in America itself.

And yet the movement towards favouring what one contemporary collection of critical essays called 'the American model' in Australian writing partly reflects the increasing Americanization of the country itself.[40] In the years of British imperial decline following World War II, Australia turned increasingly towards the emerging superpower for protection in the western Pacific from precisely the kinds of threat which Japan had posed during the war itself. As Murray himself notes in the poem 'The Smell of Coal Smoke', Japanese shells fell on several Australian cities in May 1942, including Newcastle, where his mother had been brought up (208). That sense of non-European national violation resonates behind several of the poems in the first co-authored collection, *The Ilex Tree*.[41] As a result of this new primary protectionist role for America, financial investment had increased hugely in the last years of the Menzies government, and had a massive impact on Australian social and cultural life. In gratitude for such a refocusing of defence and capital, Australia slavishly followed American policy in Vietnam, praising before other countries each escalation of the war. The anti-war protests were ineffective in changing government policy, although they did unleash a wave of political action from oppressed groups within Australia's still traditionalist society, including women's and Aborigines' groups, and ecologists.[42]

These social and economic changes are worth rehearsing since Murray's own protest against them takes more than a literary form, and underpins much of the political impetus of his

own writings in the first half of the 1970s. His 1972 collection
Poems Against Economics contains his own anti-war work. But,
as he made clear in an interview with Carole Oles, Vietnam
marked a further defining moment for him, a moment when
radicalism received 'its great spread', but also one when
'America conquered us with her left hand. ... For the first time
in Australia we saw the methods of political terorism being used
to establish hegemonies in art.'[43] From his point of view,
Vietnam marked the emergence of a new 'relegation' and
colonization, in other words. More immediately for Murray, the
emergence of the Tranter/Adamson generation as the new
literary establishment spelt the beginning of a uniformity in
style, expectation, and outlook, and a consequent exclusion from
government funding for those with his more defiant and various
interests, a result which generated a good deal of the bitterness
in some of his statements against the 'hegemony'. Much of the
more unsettling drive of some of his assumed social and political
attitudes, as in his disgust at feminism and at the economic
violation of the countryside by new mass factory methods (both
to the fore in *The Boys Who Stole the Funeral*, a novel which he
has subsequently done much to suppress himself, refusing to
excerpt it in his various *Collected Poems*), stems from understandable fears arising from this moment of Vietnam.

From this perspective, Murray's self-appointed role becomes
that of national remembrancer, undertaking a project not
altogether removed from that 'painful' task which the theorist
Homi K. Bhabha has seen as essential to forming a bridge
between a colonial past and a new cultural identity, 'a putting
together of the dismembered past to make sense of the trauma of
the present'.[44] Against the kinds of amnesia exerted upon local
culture by 'the American model', Murray asserts the (often
hazardous, fractured, awkward and even embarrassing) continuities
of putative national tradition.

And the battle over this role has been waged both ways. In a
venomous review of *Selected Poems: The Vernacular Republic*
(1976), Tranter condescendingly found Murray 'a little too self-
satisfied, a little too inexperienced in the necessarily tortured

metaphysics of the modern urban world', and accused him of 'riding on the back of superficially held assumptions'. As revealed by the title of his review, 'A Warrior Poet Living Still at Anzac Cove', Tranter sees in Murray a caricature of a *pre-modern* poet, far from the universalized postmodernism which he perceives in Australian city life.[45] For him, Murray's is the kind of idealism which fuelled the nation's first excursion as a would-be world power in its own right, the heroic but futile and disastrous landing at Gallipoli in 1915. Tranter certainly picks up here on a strong strain of rhetoric in Murray; in the passage from the preface to *The Paperbark Tree* quoted near the start of this chapter, Murray has characterized himself as having 'fought' in 'wars', both polemical and political. A consistent theme in his poetry – from 'Troop Train Returning', through 'Visiting Anzac in the Year of Metrication', *The Boys Who Stole the Funeral*, 'Aspects of Language and War on the Gloucester Road' and *Fredy Neptune* – has been a preoccupation with the historical originals of those later ideological conflicts over class and nationhood which he feels to be closely connected with them.

And yet Tranter to some extent has the wrong war here, and sets up an uncomplicated, caricatured version himself of the nature of the conflicts with which Murray has been concerned. As David A. Kent has argued in a Special Issue of *Australian Literary Studies* on Australian Literature and the War, Australia, since the federation of its states in 1901, has been 'involved in more major conflicts for more years than any other industrial nation.' The historical setting of *Fredy Neptune*, covering as it does the first half of the twentieth century through the happenstantial travels of its hero, links genocides in the World Wars I and II, as a corrective to those who only associate the word *Holocaust* with the latter. Murray's own contribution to the Special Issue, a response to a questionnaire to do with war and writing, points out the fact that 'my earliest childhood coincided with World War II, and the war atmosphere of the time got into my nascent consciousness, right down at the level of concerns which have to be faced and worked out in later life.' Yet he finds in war generally a relation with 'the human hunger for significance', seeing it as arising paradoxically 'from our longing for peace' (from what, in other words, in the early poem 'An Absolutely Ordinary Rainbow', are called the 'unexpected judgements of peace') (29).[46] In this sense of longing, he echoes again the founding ideals of Australia itself, which represented it as an idyllic land far from the conflicts which had ravaged Europe from its beginnings. 'In the year of the moonshot,' as 'The Fire Autumn' has it, on 'the column of Trajan at Rome', the 'spiralling captives continued their motionless climb' (34). Australia's distinction cannot be established without Europe's influence. Conversely, peace, which is usually equated – as the reply to this questionnaire admits – with 'tedium, mediocrity etc.', only gains significance through the thirst for war. This is a fact seemingly true for Australia's leaders, who, as Kent argues, 'have consistently shown a willingness, even an enthusiasm, to send their citizens overseas to fight in wars which seemed to have little bearing on domestic security'.

Murray's reflection of this paradox that war produces peace and peace war goes to the heart, therefore, both of his personal experience, and of that of his nation. 'What else to say of peace?' he typically asks towards the end of 'Aspects of Language and War on the Gloucester Road'. 'It is a presence / with the feeling of home, and timeless in any tense' (284). But this possible lyric resolution goes along with the counter-urge, or almost compulsion, in his writing to enter the arguments and conflicts of the moment, to engage rather than ignore what the title of a poem in *Conscious and Verbal* calls 'A Deployment of Fashion'. The only hope of a way out of this dilemma provided by his own nascent sense of the world around him, for himself and for humanity as a whole, he suggests in the *Australian Literary Studies* Special Issue, is through 'God's grace ... Without Divine grace, humans despise peace.'

Murray's reception into the Catholic Church in 1964 provides the context against which many of the (quite rare) restful moments in the later work can be viewed, although, doctrinally, Murray's faith is rarely to the fore in his poetry. Partly this must be due to his primary countering urge to establish what he sees as the true values for his nation against those who would deny or destroy them. 'Grace can't be communicated through argument', he percipiently put it in a personal appreciation for the late poet and like convert to Catholicism, James McAuley (*PT*, 68). Yet, as the obstreperous speaker of the poem 'The Say-But-the-Word Centurion Attempts a Summary', from Murray's own most deliberately obstreperous collection, the self-parodying *Subhuman Redneck Poems* (1996), says in reflecting upon Christ's sacrifice, 'regained excels kept, he taught. Thus he has done the impossible / to show us it is there. To ask it of us. It seems we are to be the poem / and live the impossible' (409). Murray's faith, therefore, quietly generates that sense of the possible and needful re-establishment of a lost integrity which informs much of his social and political argumentativeness. It gives him his vision of a creolization of Australian cultures which will allow the nation to rediscover the values which he feels underlie its founding, and also to recognize the continuities between seemingly diverse and separate strains of tradition to which it has been his often controversial role to respond.

This book will trace the emergence of these various allusions, themes, and styles as they emerge and then again recede throughout Murray's career from collection to collection. It will call upon contemporary prose by Murray where this prose illuminates and enlarges upon the poetry's emphases, and consider the various national debates into which the poetry seeks to enter itself.

This country is my mind
The Ilex Tree and *The Weatherboard Cathedral*

THE epigraph which stands at the head of Les Murray's first publication in book form, *The Ilex Tree* (1965), a collection which he co-authored with Geoffrey Lehmann, wryly offers a persona for the poet which Murray has often partially re-assumed since. 'By chance,' the lines quoted from Virgil's seventh *Eclogue* run, 'just as Daphnis had settled down in the shade / Of a whispering ilex tree, Thyrsis and Corydon came there ... / Two youths in their prime, Arcadian singers both of them, / And equally keen to make up a verse, or match one.' Through the epigraph, the eager young arrivals upon the poetry stage suggest a modesty about their work (this ilex tree is 'whispering') even as they tacitly declare their maturity with this first publication. 'In their prime', they are 'Arcadian singers both of them', concerned to sing the idealized beauties of the countryside. They are confident in the sources of their productivity, their ability either to generate their own work, or to offer a challenging response to promptings derived from earlier work by others.

This initial signal to his readership strikes a note which characterizes and underpins many of the more provocative and telling positions Murray was to assume later in his career. These have included that of a 'rural, traditional-minded' craftsman and thinker – terms he used in his debate on related matters in an essay of 13 years later, 'On Sitting Back and Thinking About Porter's Boeotia' (*PT*, 57). And such attitudes have continued to resonate through poems such as 'Crankshaft' and 'The Family Farmers' Victory' in *Subhuman Redneck Poems* (1996), where the position is often assumed with a strong combative strain. Yet even the contents of Murray's section of *The Ilex Tree* suggest how an ambitious, and latterly politicized, Arcadianism in his work is modulated and crossed by other strains, which complicate and inflect it. Nearly one-third of these poems have been retained in the revised and enlarged 1998 *Collected Poems*, not only revealing the true maturity this first book displays, but also emphasizing the complexity of the original strain itself, one withstanding (even) more mature reflection.[1]

For, from the outset, Murray's version of Arcadia is frequently a place of loneliness and despair rather than of gilded plenitude. It is also a place haunted by the ghosts of a fuller, more integrated past, when work on the land was uninterrupted by the rhythms of modern technology, or, conversely, by yearnings for the greater immediacy and facility of modern city life. Arcadia is firmly placed, in this early writing, as aspiration and ideal rather than as presence (as in truth it always was). The women in 'Driving Through Sawmill Towns', the poem which ends Murray's section in *The Ilex Tree*, when

> fetching water
> In a metal bucket will turn around and gaze
> At the mountains in wonderment,
> Looking for a city.

The 'half-heard' radios, which the women have been listening to while the men are at work in the mills, play an alluring 'song of the sidewalks'. The women's listening for 'cars on the road', for word from beyond their narrow situation, sets them apart from their untalkative, seemingly powerless, husbands, the workers in the mills:

> Men sit after tea
> By the stove while their wives talk, rolling a dead match
> Between their fingers,
> Thinking of the future. (11)

These, the closing lines of the poem, suggest that attempts *can* be made to see beyond the narrow limits of this world of Australia's Dividing Range. But that beyond is itself vague, unilluminated, for the men at least in their present situation. The perspective upon the world which this poem offers is, after all, that of an actively engaged outsider from that world beyond, in the process of 'driving through' this traditional culture. From this perspective, 'the future' is inevitably one of modernity, of the city in which such workmen's silence, however disabling, becomes a rarity. Just such a split perspective, and correlative tension between country and city, had consistently underpinned that foundational literature of Australia which provided defining instances of national distinctiveness in the bush. In Henry Lawson's story, 'The Drover's Wife', for instance, the wife of the title already reads fashion journals, and, 'Heaven help her,' takes a pleasure in the fashion-plates.

Yet 'Driving Through the Sawmill Towns' recognizes the closure of such masculine ways of life, and another poem from the collection, 'The Widower in the Country', reiterates its theme of separation and loneliness. At the same time, however, other countering poems yearn contradictorily for the regular rhythms of country existence. 'Noonday Axeman', perhaps the most achieved of these early works, sets the intermittent beat of the labour involved in felling a gum tree against modern demands and enticements. I will discuss it here as a foundational poem in relation both to Murray's personal legend, and to how he views his connection to the land. This discussion will then open this chapter's concern with the issues and themes of his early work, including the relation of the ancientness of that land to modernity, the processes of origination and individualization which Murray as a writer is involved with, and the connections between his country's vernacular speech, culture and movements of history and notions of the numinous.

> Axe-fall, echo and axefall. Noonday silence.
> Though I go to the cities, turning my back on these hills,
> For the talk and dazzle of cities, for the sake of belonging
> For months and years at a time to the twentieth century,
>
> The city will never quite hold me. I will be always
> Coming back here on the up-train, peering, leaning

Out of the window to see, on far-off ridges
The sky between the trees, and over the racket
Of the rails to hear the echo and the silence. (6)

If Murray's view of the Australian forest is imbued with something of the 'Weird Melancholy' which Marcus Clarke famously
described as distinguishing the land in his 1876 Preface to Adam
Lindsay Gordon's poems, it recognizes also that part of this
'weirdness' derives from the comparative brevity of settler
history in the Australian land. 'It will be centuries / Before many
men are truly at home in this country,' we are told. Hence the
need in this context for legends (and presumably for poems) –
'Men must have legends, else they will die of strangeness.'

For Murray, this legend is based upon a familial relation to
the land. He was later to be notably dismissive of earlier
attempts in Australian literature to consider that relation,
including the more cosmopolitan and European-literary Patrick
White's *The Tree of Man*, as 'arty falsity and inflation' (*PT*,
181). Murray substitutes instead a transgenerational familiarity
of ordinary lives and trades. The need to escape the city, forever
to 'be coming back here to walk, knee-deep in ferns', is essentially the need

> To remember my ancestors, axemen, dairymen, horse-
> breakers,
> Now coffined in silence, down with their beards and dreams,
> Who, unwilling or rapt, despairing or very patient,
> Made what amounts to a human breach in the silence.

Murray as modern axeman is of course continuing that tradition. As modern *poet*, he is making his own breach in the silence
as a commemoration of theirs. The labour of poetry becomes a
displaced but parallel activity to that of 'my forebears'. Earlier in
the poem, Murray has told us of the arrival of his 'great-great-
grandfather' on this land a hundred years before. His own
setting of the silence echoing marks a further stage in the
legend, one in which country labour forms an original and
central part, a silence to be continually retuned into: 'Things are
so wordless.'

Interestingly, however, in *The Ilex Tree* volume itself, 'Noonday Axeman' was sandwiched between the despairing monologue of 'The Widower in the Country' and 'Beside the Highway', another poem of isolation and yearning, but this time set in an impoverished Aboriginal Settlement, where all anyone can do all day is stare at walls. The boys in the Settlement dream of escaping to Queensland, but the central figure of the poem is Mad Jess, who is 'assailed by visions', including a culminating one in which '"flash cars was coming / At me like hailstones, cutting me to pieces."' (*IT*, 34). The Aboriginal Settlement, like the sawmill towns and farms of the whites in the book, seems caught between a present inanition and a modernized future of total destructiveness. The only solution seems to be that dreamt about in the next poem in the original collection, 'The Away-Bound Train'. In a couplet which has been dropped in the rearranged poem as it appears in *Collected Poems*, we are told, 'I look across the clear, receding landscape: / The price of the past is bondage to the dead' (*IT*, 36). Rather than the 'peering' towards 'far-off ridges' of the land, which confirms the potency of uncluttered rural life as in 'Noonday Axeman', here the speaker perceives only vacancy. In this particular 'timeless July', 'the cold time', the past itself is claustrophobic and entrapping, even as the present breaking from constriction cannot be immediately grasped: 'My mind / Trails far in the wake of the train.' The poem is hallucinatory in its combination of here and elsewhere. It is a combination in which the tenses of the verbs become highly slippery, as the speaker exists both in the static 'past' 'in the house' and also on the train hurtling towards a liberated future.

That double bind and self-division is, other poems in this first book intimate, partly contingent upon the anti-Arcadian version of modernity which has marked the twentieth century with its World Wars. 'The Burning Truck', the poem which Murray has set at the head of all editions of his *Collected Poems*, recalls the air raids on Perth during World War II. It offers a miraculous vision of the truck of the title, set on fire by a bomb, and running on its own through the town chased by boys, 'over the tramlines, past the church, on past / the last lit windows, and then out of the world / with its disciples' (1). This almost Yeatsian instance of a numinousness reared out of violence looks forward to later, more equivocal yet provocative, poems such as 'SMLE' from *Poems Against Economics* (1972). But, in *The Ilex Tree*, such a combination of violence and beauty has already been qualified. In 'The Trainee', which survives in the *Collected Poems*, a naive recruit sets out for World War I because of the poverty of his own life – a historical extension of the book's themes of limitation and alienation. 'A New England Farm, August 1914', 'Les paras', 'Deck-Chair Story', and 'Manoeuvres' (which, together with these other two poems, form a block about war right at the centre of Murray's section of the book) are preoccupied with the disturbing effect of violent history upon the local community and upon its sense of its own alienation. In the rural elsewhere of 'A New England Farm', the speaker sustains an innocent distance from what is being shown us – 'Why do the young men saddle horses? / Why do the women grieve together?' (*IT*, 22). The persona in 'Deck-Chair Story' recognizes not only the allure of the fantastical splendour of conflict, but also that it involves a loss of soul. More positively, in terms of Murray's Arcadianism, the person in 'Manoeuvres' comes to understand that there is a feeling of futility enforced by the nature of the landscape in which the military exercises are taking place: 'something in this country mocks our violence: / Our strength is lost on these hills' (*IT*, 27).

These unharmonious voices from the century's historical trauma resonate, then, with the more local poems elsewhere in the book that register a different futility. Most tellingly, similar voices inform the hauntedness of Murray's work here, the way in which the landscape is weirdly resonant with the ghosts of forebears. These two themes are made literal in the opening poem of the original collection, 'The Japanese Barge', in which 'A strange thing happened here / Concerning phantoms.' The ghostly barge of the title, 'queer, / Foreign', touches in to allow its phantom soldiers to disembark. The local population are led by that apparition momentarily to 'talk of battles', but, when the barge disappears again, 'drowning … / Into the dark of mind and ocean', such talk is forgotten (*IT*, 11). Japan had indeed threatened to invade in 1942, having captured Singapore. Murray's phantom imagining of this event stirs a familiar mixture of paranoia and xenophobia, curiously interwoven with that sense of strangeness and alienation to be found throughout the first collection, mingled with a recognition that the culturally other is also (paradoxically) proximate. By the mid-1960s, Australia was increasingly looking to Asia for its markets in the decline of its traditional focus on Britain. By the 1970s, Japan was the largest buyer of Australian products, 'Our Best Customer', as Murray was to put it in the title of a 1973 review.[2] Yet he controversially claimed to find that relationship, and the growing consequent Asianization of the country, a 'little easy … and at times repellent', since it was achieved through a forgetfulness of the prison camps in the war.[3]

These visionary ghostly enemies from 'The Japanese Barge', who take over the consciousness of the native population, form part of the central theme of later poems in the collection. As the speaker in 'Minuet' has it, 'I must go out. I must avoid my bed / Lately I've dreamed too often of the dead' (*IT*, 28). The World Wars which overshadow much of Murray's work, down to the experiences recounted by *Fredy Neptune* in 1998, establish here a note of inescapability and repetition, which, as I have said, serves to confirm a similar strain in other poems, where figures in the Australian landscape are seen to be irrevocably trapped. Australia's history as perceived in this early work seems unavoidably interwoven with that of the twentieth century. The legendary ghostly ancestors in the countryside suffer the same deprivation as its current dwellers, and are marked by those international wars in their turn – a theme which resonates through *Fredy*, but also through the verse novel *The Boys Who Stole the Funeral* (1980).

As a result, the foundations of the speaking voice of the poetry seem deeply unsure of themselves, not as a result of the comparative immaturity of the poet, but of the perplexities of his historical and cultural position. On the one hand, they seem self-conscious about constriction and limitation; on the other hand, they seem vulnerable to usurpation by other threatening influences from beyond, and from a modernity which disrupts connections to ancestors. The poem 'Personality' recognizes that 'the current I' of the speaker has been at odds with 'some Selves'. The authorizing cultural referents of the poem suggest both the lack of clarity in the speaker's position and the various anxieties which undermine it: 'There is a little Europe here, / A nascent continent of me ... // There is a frightened Europe here' (IT, 17). 'Privacy', the title of another poem, serves to emphasize that 'Here are three sorrows knotted into one: / Loss, July, the privacy of dreams' (IT, 14). 'Property', the second poem in the original collection, confirms the cycle of deprivation and petty revenge which follows upon the urge to keep goods protected from the world 'In my secret garden' (IT, 12). In 'Love after loneliness' and 'Agitation', love itself adds further sorrows.

Rather than manifesting an innocent Arcadianism, as signalled by the collection's epigraph, therefore, Murray's contributions to *The Ilex Tree* suggest a variety of claustrophobia, doubt and disturbance in Australian rural life that at least partly mirrors the impact upon the country of the wider conflicts of the century, as well as more recent centrings of social-economic focus. The penultimate poem in the collection, 'Spring Hail', is the most declarative in its delighted remembrance of early rural experience ('This is for spring and hail, that you may remember / A boy and a pony long ago who could fly', as the repeated refrain has it) (8–10). But, in the light of the overall tone of the poems in this first collection, the reader might be tempted to recognize also the fact that the poem's celebration of Pegasus-like freedoms emerges only after 'The beaded violence had ceased' in a distant past. An urge is established to be 'utterly gone' from the scene of revelation and celebration, rather than to be further rooted there.

More than is evident from the most successful poems which appear in the *Collected Poems*, therefore, *The Ilex Tree* originally offered a cumulative sense of 'dismay' or 'sorrow'. Its considerable poetic achievement runs counter to the disenchantments and thwartedness of the life and people it presents. The various hauntings, both personal and national, which imbue the landscape establish a sense of continuity, but continuity in hopelessness. The opposite pole to the Arcadian possibility, the modern city for which many of the country people yearn, is equally empty at its heart. Rather than accepting an unregenerate version of the pastoral, the collection offers a despairing picture of the divergent irrevocable conditions of modern life and reflects the countering pulls on people in Australia at the time. These were pulls between establishing a strong national distinctiveness and also entering a world economy from a position which broke most of the earlier identifying ties with the past.

Murray's first solo collection, *The Weatherboard Cathedral* (1969), furthered and extended some of these key themes, without finding any settled resolution to them. In this book, the poet is primarily concerned with the means of coming into possession of the land, but also with the damage which has been done to Australia by the processes both of colonization and of contemporary urbanization. In these twinned concerns, Murray's early writing picks up on themes developed earlier by Judith Wright. Yet, in a further extension of the earliest work, this collection (as its title, combining the makeshift and the grandiose in its spaces of praise, suggests) contains several poems which explore the advent of the extraordinary and potentially numinous within everyday lives. This often brings a particular inflection to the explorations of rural rhythms and attitudes, an inflection which resonates more explicitly across much of Murray's later work.

Murray's stance in the collection is very much that of an outsider to the rural life now (during 1967–68 he had lived in Wales and Scotland, and travelled for the first time in Western Europe). From this point onward, in fact, he begins to negotiate the paradox whereby his valorization of distinctive national vernacular culture in Australia is achieved whilst his writing career, his complex sense of influence, and the daily mode of his life sets him apart from those familial and cultural origins he continues to hold most dear. The opening poem, 'Evening Alone at Bunyah', finds him 'Home again from the cities of the world' (13).[4] A later poem, dropped from the Collected Poems, dramatizes Murray as ashamed 'citified stranger', gazing in upon the sweet and fertile riches of a country homestead ('The Garden Path' (WC, 36)). 'Blood', about aiding a cousin to slaughter a pig, dramatizes the unspoken hesitations and misunderstandings that arise because of the poet's seemingly having deserted life on the land:

> What's up, old son? You butchered things before ...
> It's made you squeamish, all that city life.
> Sly gentleness regards me, and I smile:
> You're wrong, you know.

The speaker's natural considerateness, in feeling that the pig could have been more humanely killed ('I should have knocked him out, poor little bloke'), is at odds with the facts of country lore ('It gets the blood out if you let them run'). And yet he is anxious to rebut any suggestion of weakness due to his move to the city, asserting rather his possession of the sacred significance of the place:

> I walk back up the trail of crowding flies,
> back to the knife which pours deep blood, and frees
> sun, fence and hill, each to its holy place.
> Strong in my valleys, I may walk at ease. (21)

The simple killing of the pig takes on, for the city-based speaker, the aura of sacrifice, demanding 'praise' for 'the creature killed according to the Law'. The grandiloquence with which the poem ends is sharply at odds with the direct description of the pig-stall with which it had opened, with the vernacular in which the cousin speaks, and with the lines on the killing itself. This confirms the distance, although on different terms, between the two men which the cousin had hinted at, yet also establishes the space for the speaker to achieve his own, more broad-ranging, reflections. These are, perhaps, intimations of that 'middle style' which Murray was later to celebrate in newspaper verse of the nineteenth century in the essay 'The Narrow-Columned Middle Ground'.

For, whatever the dilemmas suggested by this particular ending (is it a genuine response? or is the city-based poet being ironized somewhat?), the sense of the returned native standing in easy possession of his first places is repeated without irony elsewhere in this collection. 'Evening Alone at Bunyah', which reviews Murray's family's connections with the place, notoriously proclaims that 'This country is my mind' (15).[5] At the other end of the book's spectrum, in 'The Fire Autumn', which concluded *The Weatherboard Cathedral* itself, the speaker asserts the miraculous possibilities of the seasons in his landscape, both against the claims of more recent immigrants, but more particularly against the hollowness of Europe in this regard, 'beautiful but / humanized to despair':

> Like a distant coast beyond shimmer, too still for cloud,
> the trees of my forests and breakaway mountains are
>   feathering
> with gold of emergence, with claret, cerise, liquid green,
> faint blues fat with powder, new leaves clustered thick
>   down the length
> of charcoal-stiff bark.(36)

At such moments, Murray stands – as in the self-images presented by the early settlers of the country – as Adamic proclaimer of revealed possibility in this New World of 'emergence', rather than of settled meanings and established truths. What he proclaims again and again is the 'ancientness' of this land (at one with its sacrificial potential) in contrast both to Europe itself and to contemporary Australian cities ('The Canberra Remnant' presents in fractured syllabics an enclosed, scrutinized place, with 'the freez- / ing drip of Europ- / ean trees') (36). 'This is the fire autumn / in the ancient of rocks, the paradise of lost eons', as the last poem asserts (34). Another poem, 'The Last Continent', which has not been included in the *Collected Poems*, contrasts the country as it was on his great-grandfather's arrival there from Scotland with the present, where 'Deeps of the ancient forest day // Are stilled to art, and

memory' (*WC*, 49). The processes of colonization are themselves destructive, in this poem, of the primal qualities of the
land before settlers arrived from overseas. The ironically
'posthumous' 'When I Was Alive' regrets the passing of the
numinous sense of the land, when there were 'Fire and wind and
all their ancient lore / ... Before the coming of the endless town'
(*WC*, 54). 'Evening Alone at Bunyah' speaks of the 'ancient
radiance' 'Beneath this moon' (16). The poet recalls a walk
during which he threw a stone 'towards the sun / to thump
down on a knoll / where it may move a foot in a thousand years'
(14). His special affinity with the local stones ('It used to be said
that I must know each one / on the road by its first name, I was
such a dawdler') keys him into extremely gradual geological
time, set against the thrust of modern progress where 'my dark
is threatened'. It is as though the primacy of the stones in the
landscape validates their integrity and guarantees their origin,
in ways that their wry confrère the poet, himself of settler stock,
can only yearn for:

> the specific strength of a stone fits utterly
> into its form and yet reflects the grain
> and tendency of the mother-lode.

Other poems in this collection which seek to establish this
remote but primal sense of a form and rhythm from the relation
to the ancientness of the land, however, discover a more
complex and troubled experience. The astonishing primitiveness
of much of the Australian landscape might stand as an emergent
possibility in comparison to the crowded, wearied and familiar
spaces of Europe. The native fauna, as in 'Platypus', might
remain 'beneath our thoughts / To nurture difference' – even to
assuage, in its 'changeless' strangeness, the 'disjunctions' which
have crept into the nation's thinking (*WC*, 12).

Yet the landscape, whatever claims for possession are made
upon it, cannot always alleviate more personal troubles, and
might actually reveal them further. 'Recourse to the Wilderness' (the *Collected Poems* version an amalgamation of two
poems in the original collection) recalls the time of Murray's

depressive wanderings as a young man, having abandoned his BA course at Sydney, to 'the far, still Centre' (25), or to fabulous places where 'the spirits of sea-cliffs / hovered on the plain' and 'frivolous games ... sustained me like water, // they, and the is-ful ah!-nesses of things' (27). Yet, even in this Hopkinsian, primal, central existence, Murray carried guilt and visions of hell with him. As with 'The Garden Path', which speaks of 'shame that sniffs at my heels', there is a sense that the land cannot assuage personal feelings of insufficiency not remote from those shared by this Victorian poetic mentor, here and elsewhere.

These various troublings in the land come together in 'The Abomination', a poem which stands as almost a direct answer of opposite possibility to 'Blood'. A rabbit trapper makes his rounds, skirting around the intense heat of a stump-fire he comes upon near his last trap. But, eventually, he cannot escape the fire, 'a deeper fact / that stared down my evasions':

> I found
> a rabbit in my hands and, in my mind,
> an ancient thing. And it was quickly done.
>
> Afterwards, I tramped the smoking crust
> heavily in on the fire, stench and beast
> to seal them darkly under with my fear
> and all the things my sacrifice might mean,
> so hastily performed past all repair. (22)

It is as though the darkness, which in 'Evening Alone at Bunyah' Murray had feared to be threatened by the appearance of modern street lighting in his valley, is here complicit with a deeper barbarism which can never be assuaged in life or in poetry. Murray's concern with the significance of sacrifice, particularly in the human realm, forms a further central preoccupation in the 1980s, in his continuing frustration and fascination with the compulsion towards war. Here, such potential lapses into barbarism are something which must be tramped heavily under if things are to continue. In *The Weatherboard Cathedral* itself, 'The Abomination' was followed by a much less successful companion-piece, 'The Borgia Pope Relates a Painful Incident'. The pope in question has a disquieting vision of a newly unearthed statue of the pagan god Saturn suddenly bleeding, only to be brought back to everyday reality by the need to deal with 'returns / from our estates' and 'fiscal computation'(31). Once again, a system of habitual reality or belief is momentarily threatened by a more primal possibility, only for the need to suppress the incident to be immediately grasped. Ancientness, the distinctive quality of this land, appears in various forms in this collection, but is admitted as both comminatory and redemptive, both 'ah-ness!' and 'stench and beast'. Barbarousness, which is satirized in another poem, 'Susan and the Serpent – A Colonial Fiction' (in which a 'finely chiselled' colonial mother throws the charge at her blonde daughter after she has violently killed the snake invading her Eden), represents a serious underside to joyful Adamic responses to the primacy of the land expressed elsewhere (WC, 45–6). Murray is more disturbed in his relation to the land here than in some earlier work, such as 'Noonday Axeman'.

In other poems, such contradictory possibilities are directly linked to the vernacular life of the country itself. 'The Count of the Simple Shore' and 'The House of Four-X', both absent from the Collected Poems, recall events in which extraordinary but also disturbed realities are aired. In the former, 'my neighbour' gathers in his farm implements, convinced, however absurdly, that there is 'something tremendous coming'. The 'something' is 'human', but 'like history', and there is little more that the man can say (WC, 50). In the more genial 'The House of Four-X', we hear that 'Something over ten thousand / Beer bottles went to build / A house, once, in Queensland.' For the house to be swept away would, Murray claims, be 'a drear loss to us all', since we need such 'excess / … of fullness, of wholeness' (Hopkinsian 'ah-ness' again) in our lives (WC, 65–6). The poem looks forward to later works by Murray, such as 'The Quality of Sprawl', which celebrate a uniquely Australian visionary ability to go beyond the borders of the accepted, and of all limitation. Yet the preceding poem in The Weatherboard Cathedral, 'The Barranong Angel Case', had seemed to mock such vernacular displays of excessive possibility. It is frequently Murray's manner to juxtapose one poem with a contrary one throughout his work (even though the earlier collections were arranged in strict chronological order of writing). Cast as an exchange between two blokes, this poem mockingly registers varieties of local resistance to the advent of an angel in a small community ('A bit overdone, with those flourishes of wings / And that plummy accent') (*WC*, 63). Murray's scepticism towards all afflatus, understated and somewhat elusive in the case of 'Blood', here, as in later, similar, poems, receives its full dramatic expression.

This is not to say that such potentially miraculous advents within everyday life do not receive their unqualified expression in the collection as a whole, as we will see. In three extremely powerful poems, 'Once in a Lifetime, Snow', 'The Incendiary Method', and 'An Absolutely Ordinary Rainbow', single events reveal the possibility of the known world becoming the unknown. We 'might not have seen the end / of reality', as the first of these poems has it in giving Murray's uncle's response to the sudden, never-before-seen phenomenon (24). In 'The Incendiary Method', the recounted gratuitous firing of a paperbark tree sets a sixty-foot blaze going both in the actual swamp and 'in the dark of this poem', leading the speaker to reflect that 'there are more ways than one / of cleansing the spirit' (28). In 'An Absolutely Ordinary Rainbow', the narrator joins a crowd witnessing the sudden weeping of a man in a city street, a kind of blessing which quells all doubting voices and tests innocence:

> The fiercest manhood,
> the toughest reserve, the slickest wit amongst us
> trembles with silence, and burns with unexpected
>
> judgements of peace. Some in the concourse scream
> who thought themselves happy. Only the smallest children
> and such as look out of Paradise come near him
> and sit at his feet, with dogs and dusty pigeons.

What the poem celebrates, as 'Evening Alone at Bunyah' had earlier in a different register, and from the poet's own perspective, is the self-containment of the man, his 'dignity' and integrity compared to those massed to witness the spectacle:

> The weeping man, like the earth, requires nothing,
> the man who weeps ignores us, and cries out
> of his writhen face and ordinary body
>
> not words, but grief, not messages, but sorrow,
> hard as the earth, sheer, present as the sea ... (29–30)

The striking archaism 'writhen' suggests the perennial potential of this extraordinary ordinariness ('Treeroots and Earth', another poem from *The Weatherboard Cathedral*, compares the roots to 'Old writhen gods') (56). Together with the use of biblical syntax ('such as look out of Paradise'), which itself lends dignity to the poem, Murray's suggestion is that the miraculous is sudden and unexpected, and confers graceful simplicity upon the blessed. It is also elemental, bringing the recipient into tune with earth and sea, and responsible, re-establishing integrity in the disruptive city street. In that sense, it establishes an ideal wholeness within and between the twin poles of Australian life, the city and the bush, a wholeness which has been implicitly lost in this view of modern life.

'If a Pebble Fall', another poem which tests notions of the numinous against banality and a lack of primal integrity, tells of a stone dropping way down a gorge but stopping at the poet's feet rather than falling into the stream behind him. The speaker sees the incident as proof that 'the man up on top' sees 'my / Dropping out of the world' as 'my own decision', whilst restrainedly confirming the 'gravity and / Weight' of that stance (*WC*, 62). As in the opening poem of the collection, the poet's 'aloneness' seems numinously sanctioned by the 'ordinary' elements in the landscape around him. His stylistic adherence to an idiom of vernacular everydayness, and an eschewal of the 'literary', underwrites his ability to see the extraordinary events for what they are.

Several poems in *The Weatherboard Cathedral* harness Murray's outsiderness, the role which is constantly adopted throughout, to berate the banality and unthinkingness of others in this colonial situation. 'This country is my mind', as 'Evening Alone' proclaimed, but that fact allows Murray to castigate the mindlessness of others. In the ironically inflected version of the toast given in 'Prosper the Commonwealth', the scene is set at a typical cattle auction, where a neutral flow of description is rudely interrupted by the demand *'But where is the mind?'* The people in this country are

> The riverbank dead
> Pioneers even there
> The lovers and living
> The humble and proud
> Who have scant use for Mind
> Nor for Saul's armour. (*WC*, 43)

This vituperative note is struck comically elsewhere, as in 'Bagman O'Reilly's Curse', but suggests here Murray's real concern and frustration that his quest for integrity and revelation might be ignored by his countrymen. Certainly this, like other notes struck in the collection, enters a strong caveat to the potential celebrated in the collection's original epigraph, which came from Kuno Meyer's version of the Gaelic tale 'The Voyage of Bran': 'Wealth, treasures of every hue / Are in the Land of Peace – a beauty of freshness.' Australia had from early on, as Manning Clark confirms, conceived of itself as different from Europe in its freedom 'from the Old World scourge of war'.[6]

Yet that peace is again and again perceived to be untrue to lived experience. In 'Troop Train Returning' (a work which draws on a familiar theme in Judith Wright's work, as in 'Soldier's Farm', and elsewhere), the celebration of the soldiers' return to their rural lives as farmers is tempered by the fact that 'this perfect plain / casts out the things we've done' (19). In 'A Walk with O'Connor', during which Gaelic heroes, such as those contained in the epic which provides the collection with its epigraph, are recalled, any possibility of an equivalent heroic life being lived in the present is overshadowed by 'discontent', by a diminished world where the enemy can never be truly engaged, and by an inability to come close to understanding 'the Quest that summons all true men' (31). As with 'Driving Through Sawmill Towns' and 'An Absolutely Ordinary Rainbow', there is a question here as to whether manhood, the basis of many of Australia's legends about itself, is now adequate to cope with the modern world. This is a theme extended to address artistry itself, when, in 'Ill Music', a cousin's skill at the violin is shockingly contradicted as, 'touching certain chords, / he fell down, shrieked and bit at boards', a condition which leads to his confinement in a mental institution. There is speculation that the illness might be caused by 'rot' which has got into the genealogy of the family and is therefore inescapable. Such speculation is, however, beyond the afflicted cousin, Jim, since, in contradiction to his musical fluency, he now says little (18).

What these first two collections of Murray's suggest, therefore, is a complexity of experience in which the primacy of the 'Land of Peace' is obtainable, if it ever is, partly through repression, partly through miracle. Fears must remain that the past, which in many ways validates Murray's craft, but which also contains strong unease over the history of colonization and other unnamed horrors, might also thwart present activities and stifle them. Most particularly, there is a sense that modern Australia might not attend to the poet's insights, that whatever integrity and illumination he might himself obtain will be at the expense of winning any understanding from within that very vernacular culture which the poetry celebrates. 'This country is my mind', but can that country ever be made fully present to others?

Ethnic radios

Poems Against Economics, Lunch and Counter Lunch, and Ethnic Radio

IN his next collections of poetry and in his related literary activities, Murray sought to negotiate those issues of individualism and audience which had arisen through the first two books in a number of ways. He began to look more closely at the issue of the role of the artist in contemporary Australia, and involved himself more directly in the politics of the day. He also explored the mixed historical and cultural origins of the country, and began introducing Aboriginal and Gaelic models and materials more self-consciously into the writing. He gradually – and often openly in response to events including the increasing Americanization of the country – began to offer alternative models and parables of national emergence, as counterweights to what he saw as potentially decentring and disintegrative forces operating from both without and within. In this chapter I will trace these themes as they emerged from book to book, in relation also to the circumstantial material he was producing at the time.

The early 1970s saw Murray taking a more directly active role in both cultural and national politics. Spurred by a policy document on arts funding from the Australian Labor Party, which was returned to office in 1972 after over twenty years out of power, Murray published a considered but polemical article in the *Australian Quarterly*, 'Patronage in Australia'. The article served both as argument for the essential and immediate role which art should play in contemporary society, and as a demand for practical support for writers through the government's payment of a guaranteed salary. Whilst the primary focus of the article remains that of the policies of the incoming government (and lobbying like Murray's and Patrick White's proved successful, with the founding in 1973 of the Australia Council to oversee arts funding), Murray makes a universal claim for the significance of the arts:

> In a society characterised, as Western industrial society is, by *division*, art has an enormous potential value in that it is one of the very few institutions, all of them archaic in origin, whose effects are essentially *integrative*. If, however, artists are too deeply estranged from such a society, art can become a powerful disintegrative force. (*PM*, 1)

Once again, Murray has recourse to an implied parallel which had become familiar from his first two collections of poetry – that between an ancientness or archaism (often associated with the native landscape) and the crafting of works of art. And yet, as this quotation suggests, 'Patronage in Australia' is fraught with both a warning and the fear that technological and capitalist progress across the Western world might supersede and even further marginalize the arts. The resonant culminating sentences of the article suggest the possibility of a distinctive national artistic life which will be integrative of Australia's history and its well-being: 'Our governments might bear it in mind that nations are remembered for the welcome which the arts enjoyed within them. For art is the intimate memory of nations.' But such sentiments are freighted by a contrary awareness that 'the mercantile system', in Australia as elsewhere, has 'estranged' and even sought to destroy 'the archaic trades' (21). This first statement of art's claim upon the government of the day, therefore, remains sensitive to the ways in which the national qualities of Australia itself are under threat from external forces which challenge its uniqueness, as well as undermining the centrality in establishing those qualities provided by its artists.

The sense of national danger in this article then runs across both the more polemical prose pieces, and the reviews that Murray subsequently undertook throughout the 1970s, once the dam had been broken with this piece. Selected for the volume *The Peasant Mandarin* in 1978, they prove what Murray claims in the preface, that he found his delayed writing of prose 'a sovereign aid to thinking' (5–6). Many of the themes in these pieces later recur in the poetry he wrote during the decade. The theme of Australian instability had, however, already found expression in his third collection of poems published in the same year as the polemical article, *Poems Against Economics*. The collection, as the title indicates, signalled for some a more immediate involvement by the poetry with the political issues of the day than had hitherto been the case in Murray's creative work, an immediacy which was to continue in the collections from this time and beyond.

In its original form, *Poems Against Economics* opened with a section of poems called 'Seven Points for an Imperilled Star', the star being, of course, the nation as represented on the Australian flag (in 1972 also, as he tells us in an article published five years later, Murray was involved in a campaign to win a new flag, a flag more in keeping with his, and, hopefully, his country's, aspiration to become a republic).[1] This section directly plays off notions of integration, in variously appealing and criticized contexts, against those of disintegration and loss of centredness. The history of Australia and its distinguishing characteristics are, sometimes controversially, played off against various threatening forces from beyond.

'Toward the Imminent Days', the long-delayed epithalamium which opens the book, however, turns the sense of the impending loss of centre towards celebration. Typically for Murray, marriage (in this case that of his former collaborator Lehmann) comes to symbolize both continuity with the past and possibility for the future. The way in which the poet 'chooses' to remember the marriage ceremony as he paces his farm keys him into the seasonal ritual on the land, and the processes of nurture associated with it:

I am striding on over the fact that it is the earth

that holds our mark longest, that soil dug never returns

to primal coherence. Dead men in the fathoms of fields
sustain without effort millennial dark columns
and to their suspension, the crystal centuries come. (39)

Suitably, given the epigraph these two poets shared in their first
book, Murray sings of the fact that 'the Georgic furrow
lengthens // in ever more intimate country'. Poetry seems here
both at ease with itself and with the progressive farming of the
land, the leaving of human 'marks' upon it. Towards the end we
are told that 'Our lives are refined by remotest generations'.
This is writing that perceives a natural abundance that can be
harnessed for human good (sometimes with difficulty, as in the
section recalling his father struggling to calm a rogue bull) (43).
In this context, the antipathy elsewhere expressed towards city-
based progress is itself muted. Cities are 'debris driven by
explosions', but 'I love my cities too well' (41). Such sympathetic
inclusiveness ('for your wedding, I wish you the frequent image
of farms') suggests a value, both personal and broad-ranging,
within history which the subsequent poems or 'points' in this
opening section are measured against. Murray represents himself as more at ease in his role of disturbing the alien soil than
hitherto, coming close to those 'environmental values' of adapta-
tion he sees himself as sharing with the Jindyworobak poets.

'Lament for the Country Soldiers', like the later poem in
the section 'SMLE', which provides something of a personal
history of the Lee Enfield rifle, registers the disruptions of a
traditional way of life in the country caused by modern history
and mechanization. The soldiers' fighting for the 'king of
honour, louder than of England' leads the native homesteads
from which they set out to the war to be 'hacked'. Their absence
also leads to the opening of the country to what Murray
perceives as a subsequent waywardness and sterility:

Touching money, the white feather crumpled to ash,
cold lies grew quickly in the rank decades
as, far away, the ascendant conquered courage,

as we debauched the faith we were to keep
with the childless singing on the morning track. (44)

As so often in Murray, foreign wars spell a loss of integrity at home. 'Seven Points for an Imperilled Star' closes with the long occasional poem 'A Helicopter View of Terrestrial Stars', which ponders conflict at the time of the Australian government's craven support for the American involvement in Vietnam:

> By the tailed rockets' crux and criss-cross
> Who will be enemy in the crowded man's war?
>   The last creatures? The hills?
>
> We are dismissed from the stars of long contemplation
>   To fight in a running-dog war
>   Or a running-dog peace. (*PAE*, 26–7)

Such compulsions lead Murray to recall the 'old star of settlement' which founded his 'conquered island', where 'in fields / … there is a star all around you' (25). The poem ends by calling for a lost integration to be restored and a republic established. This is a republic that breaks both the colonial tie and the new economic and military dependence upon America, through a dismissal of 'Our scab of dependence the Crown' and 'the zodiac money'. He hopes that 'this hamburger consummation' may 'drive some to faith / To thinking of futures that have concurrence of trees', that they may 'look, with some failure of reticence, on into home country', where the 'dogger runs barefoot … / To dance with storekeepers' children' (27–8).

'Look from Kurnell', is Murray's appeal, which returns us to the place of the first colonial landing in Australia. In this sequence, Murray's resistance to the imperial adventure of Vietnam is a call for a republican separatism in which original perspectives are restored. Most potently, he insists that the particular values of Australian life are neglected within this overseas embroilment ('Hard to say whether the subtle sky-rim of our tenure / Or the home-paddock heart is more unexplored') (28). However, in the two poems exploring these values in this first section of *Poems Against Economics*, the available *historical* models of integration within the country are strongly questioned. 'The Conquest' recalls the arrival of the First Fleet, but focuses more particularly upon the Enlightenment values of the colony's first governor-in-chief, Captain Arthur Phillip, and his plans to civilize the Aboriginal population:

> Phillip was a kindly, rational man:
> Friendship and Trust will win the natives, Sir. (44)

Yet such benign qualities are impossible to sustain in a regime of transportation which enforces discipline amongst its own population through flogging ('The yeasts of reason work, / triangle screams confirming the widening ground') (46). Once Phillip's personal huntsman has been attacked by the Aboriginals, who are already being dismissed by the colonizers as 'pipe-smoking cretins', he turns towards a more brutal form of occupation:

> The punitive squads march off
> without result, but this quandong of wrath
> ferments in slaughters for a hundred years.

Ultimately, Murray's portrait of Phillip displays a good deal of sympathy for his ideals and for their inevitable failure ('For all the generous Governor tried to do // the planet he touched began to melt') (47). But, here as elsewhere, he recognizes the clear limitation of an approach to life founded solely upon the intellect and reason.[2] Phillip's inability to respond to the events of the moment delivers a legacy of repression upon the native population which supersedes the sufferings inflicted on the original transported convicts. Although the last poem in 'Seven Points' calls 'us' to look towards the originating perspectives of the colony, this poem calls those very ideals into question.

Similarly, in the poem which follows 'The Conquest' in *Poems Against Economics*, we find a mixed-race bushranger suffering 'justice' at the hands of a later governor. Murray's adoption of the folk form in 'The Ballad of Jimmy Governor' immediately associates his version of the story with what 'SMLE' calls 'honour, that terrible country / the poor still believe in' (50). On the morning of his hanging, this ironically named prisoner retains a natural dignity ('a man's not a rag to wipe boots on') and resignation to his fate that is at odds with the blood lust of the society people gathered to witness the spectacle ('the ladies all down from the country / are howling outside for my sake') (49). As in other poems, such as 'An Absolutely Ordinary Rainbow', the 'double aspect' of much of Murray's expression takes on here a more immediately sympathetic edge, both as rendering intimately the suffering of the bushranger and as anticipatory of responses to it. Through such means, the voice in the poem is often inherently a *dramatic* one, something that was to develop further later in Murray's career.

As Murray was to write – again about the flag issue – in 1973, the year after the publication of this collection, 'We are a vernacular culture, and the yarns, along with the accent they're told in, are our flag' (*PM*, 42). That issue of a distinctiveness founded upon the vernacular was to be developed throughout the 1970s, culminating in the twin publication in 1976 of the essay 'The Australian Republic' and a *Selected Poems* called *The Vernacular Republic*. Yet, in his earliest delineations of maverick outsiderness and of those who took on the British regime (such as 'The Ballad Trap' from *The Weatherboard Cathedral* and 'The Ballad of Jimmy Governor'), Murray is alert to the lack of ultimate success, the heroic failure, characteristic of the bushrangers. The ballad form and the particular version of local heroism celebrated within it are seen to have been finished by the despised forces of power and progress. In this sense, Jimmy Governor's being of mixed race offers both an opportunity and a cause, as Murray sees it, for a reactive racism. The distinctive vernacular culture continues as a subject culture, repressed from within the country by the forces of 'enlightenment', both contemporaneously and historically.

It is in the long sequence which forms the final section of *Poems Against Economics* that Murray seems to offer a countermovement to these 'imperilling' forces of division and invasion described in the opening seven poems (a now largely suppressed brief section of squibs, 'Juggernaut's Little Scrap-book', originally separated the two). 'Walking to the Cattle Place: A Meditation' to an extent answers the hope expressed at the end of 'A Helicopter View of Terrestrial Stars' that 'some' of the people might be driven to 'faith' and a 'look … on into home country'. The sequence's epigraph, from the Bengali writer Rabindranath Tagore, immediately establishes the tenor of the poems which follow: *'At once I came into a world wherein I recovered my full being.'* The sequence immediately manifests another return to origins, but this time one seemingly startlingly remote from that of the home country, in its recital of Sanskrit names for various stages in the life of cattle. In this evocation of a world familiar to Murray from his childhood, therefore, what we are to receive is a sense of the antiquity, but also the alienness and the variousness, of this seemingly uncomplicated world on the farm, which is an extension and re-rendition of the celebration in 'Toward the Imminent Days'. In this opening part of the sequence, Murray is also concerned to remind the Old World of Australian continuities with it, but also the renewal of possibility opened with the arrival in the New:

> To be of Europe also is a horn-dance,
> cattle-knowledge. Even here, where Europa,
> dumped rusty in her disgrace, gathered childhood afresh. (56)

What the sequence perhaps most upholds is a sense of the necessary respect which must be allotted to each creature and between species; 'birds in their title work freeholds of straw,' in this country, 'and the eagle his of sky'. These freeholds continue, however much this freedom subsequently becomes a 'Dripstone for Caesar' (57). In this context, the speaker of the sequence has 'sunk my presence into the law / that every beast shall be apportioned space / according to display' (59). This sense of the unnatural overcrowding which informs much of Murray's dislike for cities is used here to underpin an easy-going democracy, one which repeats poetically the original allotment of forty-acre plots (albeit for money) to settlers. More conclusively, there is an insistence that an upbringing on the farm, which many of those who have become successful in the modern cities of Australia share, underpins a later sense of inanition in many lives:

It will make them sad bankers.
It may subtly ruin them for clerks
this deeply involved unpickable knot of feeling
for the furred, smeared flesh of creation, the hate, the
    concern. (56)

What the sequence establishes, as signalled by the initial poem rehearsing ancient etymologies, is a sense of a prior world, one not devoid of contradictory feelings, but one which reaches back before those disintegrations which characterize modern life in the nation state.

Such continuities are related once again to the poor, those celebrated in the third poem, 'The Names of the Humble':

Far back as I can glimpse with descendant sight,
beyond roads or the stave-plough, there is a boy on cold
    upland,
gentle tapper of veins, a blood-porridge eater,
his ringlets new-dressed with dung, a spear in his fist,

it is thousands of moons to the cattle-raid of Cooley

but we could still find common knowledge, verb-roots
and noun-bark enough for an evening fire of sharing
cattle-wisdom. (58)

'Cow-talk' unites the beginnings of a culture in the Irish tale of the cattle-raid with that culture begun by the emigrants' arrival in Australia – in an earlier anticipation of that exploration of mixed or creolized origins which was to be subsequently developed in the collection *Ethnic Radio* of 1977. As the poem 'The Boeotian Count' contends, the chanting of cattle names establishes immunity from those foreign conflicts which have so shadowed the disintegration earlier in the collection: 'boys who scorn cow-talk / gladden the bayonet' (66). This 'day for the poor', as one poem says (the 'walk' starts at dawn and ends at dusk), then spins a thread whose cross-cultural resonances with Hinduism are established in 'The Commonwealth of Manu', and with African culture in the final verses. Aboriginal culture is represented in the version of nonce verses which form 'Stockman Songs'. But these shared resonances are always about the ancient rhythms established through meditation on the known local space, as the ending proves:

> The houses of humans walking home in dew-dark
> > are hillsides apart.
> As I enter my own, the moon is coming weather
> > and the sun dry honey
> > in every cell of the wood. (*PM*, 77)

What is perhaps most striking about this establishment of faith and suggestion of a just, spacious society is, however, the *performative* nature of the work, as we will see again. Murray provides an encyclopaedic rendition of terms associated with cattle, but more particularly, as the title 'Walking to the Cattle Place' suggests, places the reader inside a process of continually present engagement. A lot of the language and the technical terminology has an estranging effect, but that is to the purpose of the perspective drawn in the sequence, one which challenges the known contemporary world and suggests alternative potentials to those derived from Western history. The language of the poetry performs this distance from the known and the established. As a result, 'Walking to the Cattle Place' provides the most successful, complex and sustained engagement with Murray's own childhood, with faith, and with the issues of integration in his country that he had produced to date. It is both inside his own experiential perspective and beyond it, placing it within a wider imagined and integrative cultural and historical possibility.

The first edition (1974) of Murray's *Lunch and Counter Lunch*, published by Angus and Robertson, bore on its back cover the Southern Cross flag, the colours of which had been altered by the poet. This flag had been flown at the Eureka stockade in the mid-1850s, when diggers raised an insurrection against the government, which was seeking to impose impoverishing licences upon them for their gold-mining. As such, as Murray tells us in 'The Flag Rave', 'it may be too heavily freighted … to serve as the flag of a united nation.' And yet, in his re-coloured version, with a red cross inside a white on a blue field, he felt that it retained the suggestion of the emblems of the French and American revolutions, 'the flags of our colonial past. At the same time, therefore, it '[made] a distinctive new emblem for the future.' In the essay, he claims that he sees many things in this design for a putative republic's flag – 'the sacred-site diagrams of the Aborigines ... horizons ... and wheatfields, and grassland and rivers' (*PM*, 242–3).

This unifying vision is also carried forward by the book's original blurb, which claimed that

> In a time of social division, one-eyed allegiances and fervid over-simplifications, Les Murray's is a thoughtful, many-toned voice. His poetry sparks across fissures in society. ... Intensely Australian, and unwilling to break faith with the promise of the New World, he unearths new riches from the lives of many different sorts of people.

This is the most direct expression of the poetic and political ambition of Murray's project to date, the suggestion that it might offer the country a new possibility founded upon the insurrectionary elements in its past, but also one aware of the inescapable colonial heritage. The 'many tones' of the poetry will reflect the many voices to be heard in the nation, but the poetry will also stand as something else, a vision of the ways in which those voices might be brought together in a new state.

Given this, the book's opening poem, 'Dedication, Written Last: For the Vernacular Republic' (later entitled 'The Mitchells'), initially comes as something of a surprise in its quietness and reticence:

> I am seeing this: two men are sitting on a pole
> they have dug a hole for and will, after dinner, raise
> I think for wires. (117)

The voice is curiously uncertain of itself; the hiatus in labour provided by the lunch break echoes the stillness of the scene (we are back here in the particular space celebrated in 'Noonday Axeman'). The only sounds initially are the hum of bees and water boiling for tea. Only at the end of the octet do we *overhear* something which might be pertinent to the poem's title, '*drought*

that year. Yes. Like trying to farm a road.' True, the statement
carries that 'triumph of restraint and improvisation, of the
sardonic', which, in 1975, Murray hoped were qualities still
'deeply Australian' (*PM,* 100).³ The poem offers identity
through family; the men associate themselves with, and define
themselves through, their name. Their speech, we are told, is
ritualized, and seems true of both town and country, since we
might overhear it also in a built-up avenue.

This characteristic restraint and reticence are of course
something which has particularly marked Murray's own
practice as a poet. In the review 'Flag Pieces' (1973), he had
expressed a desire, dependent upon his 'country training'
perhaps, 'to celebrate something, without giving it away. It may
be a paradox, but I dream of someday reading, or writing, a
richly secretive book' (*PM,* 43). If he has not produced that book
yet, there is a secretive, riddling quality to some of his work
which is connected to this form of celebration. The identity of a
machine in 'Machine Portraits with Pendant Spaceman', from
The People's Otherworld (1983), for instance, is guaranteed to
leave the reader 'beetle-browed' (194); 'Inside Ayers Rock',
from *Subhuman Redneck Poems* (1996), it gradually emerges, is
ironically about a petrol station, and not the national landmark
(435). The obliquity of Murray's poetics, as in its refusal to
declare its own subject matter, is intimately attached to what he
sees as national withholding, signalled also in the snatched
vernacularism of 'The Mitchells'.

What is striking here is the *inactivity* of the scene in the
poem, however, the sense of an in-between time and uncertain
location, which mirrors the uncertain status of the nation itself,
between a colonial past and an envisaged future, the unrealized
'vernacular republic'. The Mitchells themselves noticeably assert
nothing, whilst the tense of the poem is that of a continuous
present. We have to make sense of their language for them, as
though the vernacular itself has not yet grown to full expressiveness of its own culture and experience. Such historical and
temporal considerations might themselves be qualified by
Murray's assertion in his essay 'The Australian Republic' itself

that 'much of our national timidity and frustration as a people stem from an inhibition in language: we keep snubbing ourselves out of speaking the liberating word' (*PT*, 45). Further, the poem's sonnet form does suggest modest containment rather than garrulous assertion.

In the poem which originally followed this 'Dedication', the strikingly non-vernacular 'L'esprit de l'escalier', the speaker meditates on the ways in which there is often a delay before finding the perfect riposte to someone's assertion:

> It's good, though, this ligament
> its extremity makes poets as often as monsters
> self-assertion turned back on itself
> enough times, may breed culture.
> Take
> Elizabeth Bowen's candour: *I resolved*
> *never again to be at a disadvantage.* (*LCL*, 2)

Whereas the dedicatory poem had seemed to suggest that the citizens of the vernacular republic were by nature reticent, this more society-based poem seems to suggest in parable form that reticence itself, or at least tongue-tiedness, allows a space in which contrary self-assertion can grow – a lesson presumably for the nation at large as well as for the individual speaker. In the space between the colonial and the later nation, *'disadvantage'* might be overcome. In 'Pentecostal', the subsequent poem from the opening of the original collection, another speaker, 'Coming away from a modern occasion', voices his resentment:

> I was ground all my life between the levels of language,
> by liberal English, our Worldspeak, that horrible binary
> code of left/not-left, stylish/unstylish.

As a result of that intractability, he imagines a truly Pentecostal leavening, in which a long-held 'dear sense' gives way to another language: 'they are angels, of human-instinctive feather, these unassuming / verberations' (*LCL*, 4–5). This launch into unknown words offers a God-given speech as an unbinaried, distinctive colloquialism. 'We are a colloquial nation,' as in the later poem 'Cycling in the Lake Country', 'most colonial when serious'

(106). Murray's in-between temporality here and consequent 'verberation' identify on their own terms that 'mimickry' and hybridity which Homi K. Bhabha has established as the particular energies within postcolonial writing.[4]

Out of its own established oppositions (*Lunch and Counter Lunch*), therefore, what this collection seems more focused upon than Murray's earlier work is the offering of parables of national emergence and especially of an abundance overcoming limitation. The beans described in 'The Broad Bean Sermon' start off as 'in any breeze ... a slack church parade / without belief, saying *trespass against us* in unison'. And yet, having suffered a visitation from heaven correlative to the gift of tongues in 'Pentecost', they are transformed prodigiously:

> Upright with water like men, square in stem-section
> they grow to great lengths, drink rain ...
>
> like edible meanings, each sealed around with a string
> and affixed to its moment, an unceasing colloquial
>   assembly
> the portly, the stiff, and those lolling in pointed green
>   slippers. (112–13)

What we are being taught here is not to assume that the repressed and meek will not inherit the earth, break free from history, and find their own time ('affixed to its moment'), in a multitudinousness which overwhelms the traditional constraints of poetry and of written English generally. Elsewhere, this is a cause for troubled concern, a continuing recognition of the possibilities of cultural debility when writing against the 'Worldspeak' of English. As the sequence 'Cycling in the Lake Country' also has it,

> No ruins in Australia?
> Here are the ruins of seas
> and ruins in the mouth:
> the place-names here are now
> pronounced in English. (103)

The English-writing Australian poet's task, as exemplified by this sequence, becomes therefore a matter of retrieval and reconnection, establishing links between the imposed but locally broken colonizer's language and the realities of the country which have been suppressed. Like the pioneers discussed by Paul Carter, the lapsing of the inland sea leaves Murray with the task of recovery and *naming* itself, establishing the ignored places on the map as realities. This is achieved through the present metaphor of journeying, as it had been from the start in Murray ('Driving Through Saw Mill Towns'). Indeed, all of these works elevate the notion of present travelling into a freedom which can unite both the indigenous population of Aborigines and the settlers. This is at the heart of the naming taking place in 'Cycling in the Lake Country':

> The free-leaping spirit
> hunters and white men with wheels
> have one fact in common:
> heat, flies and self-doubt
> fall away from a man dressed in speed. (104)

One way of going beyond reticence towards self-assertion, in all senses, therefore, is to keep on the move, to escape, as another poem of naming, 'Escaping Out There', has it ('There are no people now at Praising White Moth Larvae') (99). The immediate adjectivally based, *present tense* nature of this elusive poetics is its point. Freeing oneself of the constrictions of history (or History) is a way of establishing a new connections and separate identities. As 'Escaping Out There' concludes,

> My name will rub off out there on the lips of the
>   watershed
> and when I am fine as cloud-webbing, I will drift
> vaguely down valleys,
> me, or my water, if it comes to that,
> into further lives
>
> I will make good ancestors. (100)

The seeming temporal confusion of that last phrase captures fully the sense of needing to establish a different tradition and a new temporality within the nation and the language. Whilst the speaker of this poem is in himself remote from the poet, the resonances of such an escape are obvious for what they suggest about a founding poetics in the New World. As James Joyce, skewly evoked in the title and attitude of 'Portrait of the Autist as a New World Driver', also recognized, the way of writing in and of a colonial situation is to 'fly by' the nets entrapping you, most especially the nets of language. As Murray says in his 'Portrait',

> Under the overcoming
> undiminishing sky you are scarcely supervised:
> you can let out language
> to exercise, to romp in the grass beyond Greek.
> You can rejoice in tongues,
> orotate parafundities. (101)

The pentecostal here comes to save and elevate the naturally reticent and oppressed speaker into a play of language which is beyond the known. Murray calls himself a 'half-autistic kid' again in the later 'The Shield-Scales of Heraldry' from *Subhuman Redneck Poems*, a telling and moving self-appellation given that the collection also contains a poem for his own autistic son. Given a break from the nightmare of history, he seems to assert, the repressed might take over and change the language. Such (literally) rejoiced abundance, a sense that the known order can easily be overwhelmed, finds its most angry parable in *Lunch and Counter Lunch*, perhaps, in 'Thinking About Aboriginal Land Rights, I Visit the Farm I Will Not Inherit'.

Murray's father had had the family farm willed away from him to a cousin through his own father's unjust dislike (something later addressed in 'Three Poems in Memory of My Mother'). What the poem suggests is the tenuousness of all settlements made upon the land, which is not to say that the land rights, which were concurrently being discussed in Australia's parliament, are not at the root of all national justice:

> The ambient day-tides contain every mouldering and oil
> that the bush would need to come back right this day.

And yet Murray's response to this potential flowing-in of nature upon the settlement is not, as elsewhere, to establish his own kind of escape and freedom. Instead, 'I go into the earth near the feed shed for thousands of years' (93–4). In the essay 'The Completed Australian', the poet suggests that the issue of ownership of the land was a further link between the poor white settlers and the Aboriginals, 'a blurring of conceptual apartheid between the two' (*PM*, 98). At this level, the 'ruins of Australia' takes on a more immediate political charge, one which the subsequent collections were to consider more fully.

This contest over inheritance through the male line, however, raises another central concern within the oppositions at the centre of *Lunch Counter Lunch*, that of a threatened masculinity. 'Portrait of the Autist as a New World Driver' had, despite the gender of this free-wheeling artist, offered a contentious gendering of his situation ('if you asked / where the New World is, I'd have to answer / he is in his car / he is booming down the highways'). And yet, throughout the collection as a whole, despite this inspirited celebration and the 'Dedication' with its own portrait of reticent Australian manhood, the issue of maleness seems a fraught and uncertain one. 'The Police: Seven Voices' offers its firm reposte to the *literary* and aesthetic version of authority handed down through the modernism of T.S. Eliot (*The Waste Land* deriving its original title from Dickens's 'He Do the Police in Different Voices'). Murray's police are thoroughly modern and also thoroughly brutal ('*With strong lights to shine through hard men / and hoses – men have died fighting those ... / Men have died of falling down stairs / have ruptured their spleens eating pies*') (81). The third poem in the sequence, 'Discontent, Reading Conan Doyle', which is voiced by a snide detective, seems, against this real violence, to lament between its lines the loss of an older 'police': 'After the age of belief / we're what happened to mystery' (82). And yet at the same time we can sense the unease from the poet at this social model of righteousness ('Let us touch our forelocks').

What we find elsewhere in the book instead of praise for such gentlemenly virtues is the attractive but debilitating riotousness of the Murray male ancestors. In the (again) ironically titled 'Their Cities, Their Universities', we are recalled to the Scottish inheritance of the family through the whisky-fuelled binges the male ancestors resorted to on great occasions. These events established their own rhythms through the fiddle music and the recitations of Burns that went on ('the patriarchs are keeping their own time'), but also established the penury of the subsequent family, because of the patriarch's gambling and drinking away of their inheritance. It was a circle which excluded women, but, as he wrote elsewhere, the binges bequeathed their own awkward models to subsequent Murray males:

> This left me, like many of the generation just before mine, with both a certain nostalgia for the wealth we might have had if our grandfathers had held on to their land and a lasting fear of induced madness, of all false glamours and disarray. This fear makes our native moral snobbery all the more pronounced. (*PM*, 76)

But that fear seems also to have bequeathed a sense that circumstances and history might emasculate the contemporary male, particularly one who sought to 'better himself', to escape the family 'fears', through the education which became more available after the war. In the 'spiral of sonnets' recalling his own anguished days at the University of Sydney, 'Sidere Mens Eadem Mutato', Murray is preoccupied by this notion of a reduction of maleness:

> Literate Australia was British, or babu at least,
> before Vietnam and the American conquest
> career had overwhelmed learning most deeply back them:
> a major in English made one a minor Englishman. (109)

There seems another fear here, that the colonizers offer a more effective masculinity than that available to Australians, a nation which, as the collection's 'Dedication' had after all again reminded us, founds its distinctiveness upon a version of maleness. As in 'Aqualung Shinto', which recalls the attempts by divers to recover wreckage from some of the Japanese fleet sunk off Australia in World War II, there is some fascination with 'tracing down' figures like 'an Imperial captain' or with the troops holed up in jungles years after the war. As one of the voices of the divers given in the poem says, '*What withers us is that Australia / is a land of shamefaced shrines'* (92). Or, in the 'spiral of sonnets', those of 'our elders' who in the late 1950s and early 1960s turned in imagination, thought and spirit, 'like unlicensed guns', to the university ideal of advancement did not foresee the outcomes,

> like being called the Masses, Funny Little Men
> who live in the Suburbs and resemble Eichmann. (111)

As elsewhere throughout this book, male power is somewhere in the past, displaced, and also often brutal and sinister. The implication in this hiatus collection is that it might re-emerge into a new colloquial possibility, which, however, seems doubtful and undefined. For all of the original back cover's proclamation of a newly unified independent state, this is a work which often confronts the uncertainties and 'ruins' on which it is to be built. It marks a moment of clear doubt in the wake of Vietnam and of cultural shifts throughout the 1960s, a wondering about the definition a new nation might take.

The *Ethnic Radio* volume (1977) offers, if anything, an even more intense and elaborate exploration of the various traditions of the country which Murray felt would need interweaving, were a republic to emerge (the government had established a network of so-called ethnic radios from major cities in the mid-1970s, broadcasting to a range of different cultural groups, as a mark of recognition of the increasing diversity of the population). Murray's 'take' on this is contentious, as ever, in that he reinflects 'ethnic' to include strains of lineage within the white, English-speaking, population. Whilst the book establishes and exploits again the flexibility inherent in the English language, and its vernacular energies, it also focuses upon other forms of inheritance from the Celtic/Gaelic strands, brought over by Scottish and Irish convicts and settlers, as well as the indigenous strands from the Aborigines. To this extent, as the central sequence, 'The Buladelah-Taree Holiday Song Cycle' (its own form derived from Aboriginal models), suggests, the book takes its own break from the pressures of standard English poetic forms. Indeed, the whole book, as it was originally packaged in the Angus and Robertson edition, advertized this possibility on its cover and title-page, both of which bore elaborate Celtic designs. The work was therefore intent upon tuning in to those influences which had formed Murray's distinctive perspective upon the language he speaks.

In a review of 1974, 'The Lost Inheritance', Murray spells out for the first time the significance of what was shortly to become a central resource for his poetry. Whilst acknowledging that Gaelic is no longer spoken in Australia, he asserts that those from Gaelic or other Celtic families continued to reveal the shadows of the tongue's essential features:

> Many of their attitudes, even their turns of phrase, were only really comprehensible in terms of that lost inheritance. Their education had been concerned with other things and had failed to draw out and elucidate the elements of their past for them. (*PT*, 18)

Murray's own consciousness of the tradition, therefore, enables him to mount a further attack upon a modern schooling which he has consistently felt is alien to most Australians' true concerns. It also, in this instance, enables him to distance the culture of his country from that of Britain. Whilst acknowledging that 'English law, English tradition, English literature' have been 'central in forming our culture', he feels that their continued study in Australia is part of 'a colonial hangover'. Rather, his people should return to thinking through their particular inheritance, for 'from the beginning white Australians have been an Anglo-Celtic rather than an Anglo-Saxon people'. The Gaelic/Celtic strand in Murray's own background, therefore, offers him an immediate model for that sense of continuity which he often seeks (in a review of the next year, he proclaims himself to be 'too Gaelic-minded', perhaps, to 'admire' 'rootless modernism') (*PT*, 40). And yet, as he also writes slightly later, whilst the Gaelic inheritance must be recovered if the colonial temperament is to be thrown off, it must not in itself become a dominating strand of the New World culture, since 'It ... belongs to the past. We aren't Europeans any longer: some of us never were' (*PT*, 53).

Ethnic Radio, despite its literally Celtic trappings, reveals its own alertness to such complexity, and to the stranglehold which any attachment to a singular version of origin might exert. Indeed, at the outset of the collection, that whole theme of inheritance is complicated in ways which recall the uncertainties with which it was treated in *Lunch and Counter Lunch*. Murray is all too aware of the 1974 review's sense of 'loss' in many contexts. 'The Euchre', which stood at the head of the original edition, calls up those drink-fuelled card-playing scenes in which his forefathers lost their farms. Towards the end of the book 'Cowyard Gates', in which he visits the ruin of his own childhood farmhouse, reveals a similar loss of rootedness. On a more general level, 'Lachlan Macquarie's First Language', which had originally stood as the second poem in the book, openly questions whether the vision of the early governor-in-chief of the colony, the man who brought unity and purpose to it (an 'upright man' as Manning Clark calls him), has been fulfilled.[5] Macquarie's 'first language' was not English, but the Gaelic of the island of Mull where he was born, and Murray's poem therefore offers itself as a translation:

What like were Australians, then, in the time to come?
                ... Had they become a nation?
They had, and a people. A verandah was their capitol
though they spoke of a town where they kept the English
    seasons. (116)

The respondent to Macquarie's imagined questions suggests that the yoke has not been thrown off, and, further, that although most Australians have become, to whatever end, 'ladies and gentlemen' (so abolishing the divisive class barriers which have distorted Australian history), there is much that cannot be understood from the founder's perspective. This lack of understanding includes, not least, what seems a recollection from the poet's own early life where he is urged to trade rabbit skins for copies of Bugs Bunny comics. The oblique style of this is very much to the poem's point. The confusion of past and future tenses suggests the distance of the tradition Macquarie's idealism sprung from to that of mainstream English imperialism. And yet, in its own incomprehensions, it suggests also the remoteness of the 'first language' from the subsequent history of the country. Maquarie's is literally a lost language there, and his ideals are to a certain extent lost as well.

These trends come together most personally and intensely in *Ethnic Radio*'s 'Elegy [originally the more Gaelic 'Lament'] for Angus Macdonald of Cnoclinn'. MacDonald, as a note in the original collection tells us, was perhaps the last Gaelic *seanachaidh*, or remembrancer, and 'with him died a tradition of oral learning going back to the days before the Roman Empire' (*ER*, 62). Macdonald's students including Murray received from him, the poem suggests, a vision of life which was also quintessentially Australian in its strangeness, an ancient ideal of 'the harmony of the men of peace'. He enabled them to 'haul from the conqueror's sea / of myth, our alternative antiquity'. As a result, although he clearly feels guilty of some betrayal of Macdonald in not carrying on the dying tradition himself and writing poems in Gaelic, Murray rises to his own form of self-assertion: 'I am not European. Nor is my English ... / in the new lands, everyone's Ethnic / and we too, the Scots Australians / ... may recover ourselves, and put off oppression' (152–3). Murray cannot carry forward the truly different language (wryly he reports that his claims to have written 'Gaelic in English words' made Macdonald sniff and smile), but the loss of his friend leads him into a fresh assertion of his ancestry, an ancestry at one with Macquarie's own. As he was to note in his extended discussion of his ancestry, 'The Bonnie Disproportion' of 1980, Scots Australians form part of a clannish, 'extended-family' sense of connectedness disallowed to other racial groups:

> It is a powerful sheet anchor for a threatened identity, to possess a blood tie, not genealogical in the linear feudal way but ramified and tribal in a Gaelic way, with a quirky assortment of noble and sometimes poignant figures inhabiting distant centuries. (*PT*, 121)

The intermixing of high and low obviously provides him with one model for the distinctive republic. Yet he is constantly alert, in this collection as elsewhere, to the fact that Australia's history and culture, like others, allows few opportunities for actual movement between social strata and different racial or 'tribal' worlds. The issue of translation, the ways in which these now lost languages, including the Aboriginal, have come over and reinflected Australian English, is at the centre of this collection. 'Employment for the Castes in Abeyance', which recalls Murray's time from 1963–67 as a scientific and technical translator at the Australian National University, delights in the fact that, for all their efforts, the scientists have been unable to develop a translation program for computers:

> If they could be taught not to render, say, *out of sight out of mind* as *invisible lunatic*
>
> they might supersede us ... (134)

More significantly, perhaps, the poem celebrates the bizarre mixing of cultures which working in the institute introduced him to, a mixing which offered in miniature the creolized nation as a whole ('Prince Obolensky succeeded me for a time / but he soon returned to Fiji to teach Hebrew'). What seems to have developed during this period in Murray's career is a more declarative sense of the ethnic multiplicity of the emerging nation. The land rights issue was clearly one impulsion towards this, although Murray had been set to edit an anthology of translated Aboriginal verse in 1970. That multiplicity then provided him with alertness to the variously derived models to be found in his work, here and later. 'The Flying-Fox Dreaming' and the holiday song cycle openly display their 'origins' in Aborigine works, such as the transcribed oral works and the 'Song Cycle of the Moon-Bone', translated by R.M. Berndt, which Murray was to collect in his *New Oxford Book of Australian Verse*. Once again, a freedom from the constraints of daylight consciousness and from the mundane labours of 'employment' is presented as an escape into a present-tense writing which is carried over into English from Berndt's versions. The cycle represents a 'holiday' from standardization, in which unusual content, such as the string of place-names in the song cycle, can be included. Murray, in introducing the collection of his prose pieces *Persistence in Folly* (1984), points out that, 'As many have demonstrated, the dreamworld is a frequent and natural place for whites and Aboriginal Australians to meet' (2).

The poetic 'dreamworld' of *Ethnic Radio* itself provides such a place. Murray's vernacular republic, as it emerges in this collection more intensely than before, takes into account a variety of inflections and oralities, from the Gaelic to the Aborigine. This alters the pace and the rhythm, as well as the tense of the poetry:

> Forests and State Forests, all down off the steeper country;
>   mosquitoes are always living in there:
> they float about like dust motes and sink down, at the
>   places of the Stinging Tree,
> and of the Staghorn Fern; the males feed on plant-stem
>   fluid,
>   absorbing that watery ichor;
> the females meter the air. (142)

Through such passages as this, from the eighth section of 'The Buladelah-Taree Holiday Song Cycle' (Taree being the place of Murray's own schooling), that 'ritual' element in Australian speech noted in 'The Mitchells' takes on a wider resource.[6]

In 'The Australian Republic', Murray had seen such holidays and days of national celebration (lushly reviewed in his 1985 commentary to the photobook *The Australian Year*) as evidence that

> the republic already exists and has indeed existed for a long time … [It] is inherent in our vernacular tradition, which is to say that 'folk' Australia, which is the real matrix of any distinctiveness we possess as a nation, and which stands over against all of our establishments and colonial élites. (*PT*, 46)

Whilst the essay is fraught with the sense that vested interests, including monarchists and 'the educated classes', are in a position of 'all-out war' with vernacular Australia, *Ethnic Radio* shows a defiant sense of the complexities involved in that 'folk' world. There is a shared set of ideals between the poor farmers in the bush, the Aborigines in their quest for land rights and a true acceptance of their original cultural inheritance, and those whose Celtic inheritance is being suppressed by other predominant forces within White Australia.[7]

The extended lines of Murray's holiday song cycle themselves look forward to 'The Quality of Sprawl', which underpins the poetics of the next two books. But here, in their mapping of the land through its sacred places and its native flora and fauna (something which happens in less culturally engaged terms in poems like 'The Returnees', 'Creeper Habitat' and 'Spurwing Plover'), Murray suggests that there is some consonance between that continuous present-tense poetry he had celebrated in *Lunch and Counter Lunch* and the oral works and dreamworld of the Aborigines. The lake being rowed across in 'The Returnees' has 'far ancient hills under it ... / it was the light of Boeotian art' – recalling the terms of Murray's famous debate with Peter Porter. And yet that art itself has much in common with the Aboriginal, it is implied. 'Laconics: The Forty Acres', which celebrates the fact that Murray had eventually managed to get the family farmland back by buying it, sees him settling to a land 'husbandry' which draws all traditions on the soil together:

> Our croft, our Downs,
> our sober, shining land. (129)

'The Gallery', a few poems later in the book, seems momentarily to raise questions similar to those of the first poems there. The underground rock formations beneath the local fields open up a space for self-questioning once more ('rock-bench of basalt / do we know anything yet?'), before re-emerging to a fruitful land level at the end ('the daylight moon ... / is putting on flesh / and seeds.') (133–4). But, more generally, the tuning into different ethnic origins, however necessarily awkwardly translated, shows Murray more settled in his sense of integrative poetic, and potentially national, possibility.

The original final poem in the book, 'The Figures in

Quoniam', had even seemed to present a model of interlacing correlative to that which had held in its earlier renditions of the elaborate Aborigine song cycle. Brooding on the capitals in the Book of Kells, their blendings of an imperial Latin with a native art, Murray discovers 'integrations' between languages and the world, 'the speech of words and the speech-that-is-not-words'. This provides him with a sense of an ideal, equitable otherworld, which will resonate throughout his next book:

> I rejoice most of all in this insight ...: Hell, Purgatory,
> Limbo, sociability, Ascent, are all shown in one field
> with a steadily upward movement. (*ER*, 62–3)

In other words, the Book of Kells provides a further model for an emergent republic. It also has no foreground and background, such as (in 'Equanimity' in the next book) Murray was to see as a specific feature of natural grace in Australia and of God's 'attention'. What is interesting in this collection, which, after its opening poems, seems more assured in the poetic models it can draw upon for its own acts of 'integration', is that (perhaps with the buying and regaining of the farm at Bunyah) some of the anxieties discovered in *Lunch and Counter Lunch* are largely allayed. 'Visiting Anzac in the Year of Metrication' would seem to be about to offer a parable of the ways in which subsequent belittling government regulation had blighted the founding achievement of Australian folk heroism at Gallipoli. In fact, despite its recognition of the horrors of the battle, and of the haunting of subsequent national history ('a nation stalled in elegy'), the poem ends with a distancing manoeuvre, one which seems accepting of the loss of such achievements to time:

> Those shelterless hardscrabble cols
> where even the Heads get *knocked* were best
> assaulted in youth: we were handiest,
> the climbing was overt and in vogue
>
> and done with friends, in company. (122)

The tone of this is surprisingly laconic, suggesting that the pioneering fighters were simply following a (however terrifying) fashion. Whatever the criticism of contemporary government made in comparison to this action, or the perceived destruction of local relationships which that action had itself involved, Murray seems finally remote from that world. He is also remote from the models for the nation which the government might have offered.

After the variously direct political engagements which the collections of the 1970s had made, we see him emerging at the end of the decade with a more resolved sense of the poetics upon which he could combine various strands of tradition into a vision of a new nationhood, one potentially operative despite the injustices and follies of the ruling and academic classes. In this, he takes his own (and his nation's) multiple experience of dispossession and maps them onto other losses evident in the country's history, in order, as he contentiously but inclusively puts it, that 'we might recover ourselves, put off oppression.'

God bless the general poetries?

The Boys Who Stole the Funeral,
The People's Otherworld, The Daylight Moon
and *Dog Fox Field*

IN Murray's next works, those models of integration which he had sought to define at the political level in recent books took on a more religious and metaphysical tone. *The Boys Who Stole the Funeral* redirects some of the earlier Aboriginal material relating to the sacredness of place in a new light, but subsequent collections open out notions of the spiritual in other ways. Whilst remaining preoccupied by themes such as connection to the cycles of the land, and the relationship of Old World to New, Murray now undertook a more literally speculative enquiry into questions of vision and perspective. He also took up, at both more personal and more general levels, considerations related to social justice, and ecological concerns raised by the era of international capitalism, which was taking deeper effect in Australia. More specifically, throughout the next decade of his career he was seeking a formal basis for the notions of national distinctiveness which he had developed earlier, and considering also the relation of that national form to his own work. These developments will be reviewed in this chapter.

Murray began the 1980s with a change of formal direction. Sequences of the 1970s like 'Walking to the Cattle Place' and 'The Buladelah-Taree Holiday Song Cycle' had revealed his interest in more expansive poetic lines, forms, and spaces that allowed for multi-angled shots at a subject. Works like 'Visiting Anzac in the Year of Metrication' and 'Aqualung Shinto' showed him weighing his relation to history in longer meditations than the lyric. 'Their Cities, Their Universities' and, perhaps more appropriately here, the 'spiral of sonnets' 'Sidere Mens Eadem Mutato' had seen him considering his own past through a series of related poems. *The Boys Who Stole the Funeral*, the novel sequence in a variety of sonnet forms, which appeared in 1980, takes up this formal interest in the most concerted way. In over 130 poems, the variations carry the narrative of two young men who seek to fulfil the wishes of a dying Anzac soldier that he should be buried back in his home district, and not in the alien city where he lives. The book is, perhaps as a result, extremely uneven in quality, and Murray has consistently excluded it from gatherings of his best work. The novel also raises issues of politics and belief which make many readers deeply uneasy, since its central human and sympathetic story of reclamation and spirituality is surrounded by angry attacks upon various trends in contemporary society.

In his brief essay 'Notes on the Writing of a Novel Sequence', Murray has laid down some of his impulses in putting the story on paper. Despite its elaborate formality, he claims, the origins of the work lay 'essentially' in 'the storytelling methods I unconsciously learned from my father in my childhood – Dad is a man whose culture is almost wholly oral and musical.' As such, Murray sees the formal departure as establishing a distance between his work and that of 'the grey, conformingly non-conformist tone of modern poetry … I was further than ever from acquiescence in its received class values, or from playing little timid variations on them.' One aim of the book, therefore, is to recapture something of what Murray sees as the origins of poetry itself in narratives which *all* people might understand and have access to. In another of the rebuttals of 'Modern Literature' which Murray was to make throughout his career, he makes it clear that his rejection is founded upon his sense of its class exclusion, and his own at-one-ness with the 'despised and relegated poor, the people I come from and belong to'. The social and spiritual origins of *The Boys*, as Murray sees them here, are – in line with those of *Ethnic Radio* – cross-racial, but continuous with this emphasis on his own origins:

> I mused about ... the serious value which is attached to
> funerals in the Australian rural culture from which I come
> ... I thought, too, about the vital importance for many
> Aborigines of returning a person's remains to their parti-
> cular spirit country so that their soul may be reincarnated
> when a pregnant woman passes by. (PT, 139–41)

The verse novel sequence plays strongly upon these
perceived relations between two cultures and traditions. The
story of the transportation of the body of Clarrie Dunn from the
funeral home in Sydney to the mountains behind the north
coast interweaves elements of rural intuition – as when Clarrie's
nephew Athol realizes in a dream that the boys are about to pass
his farm with the body – with a more expansive and culminatory
exposition of Aboriginal rituals concerning rock crystal, through
which the individual might come into his own destiny. One of
the boys, Reeby, is killed near the end in an altercation with the
police, and his colleague Forbutt undergoes a rite of visionary
homecoming and cleansing with Aborigine guides. To this rite
Murray then adds an invention of his own, the Common Dish
from which all eat, as an emblem of the shared need and
recourse of humanity.

The story is further presided over by the intermittently
present 'burning man', or 'whistle-cock man'. This figure focuses
some of the themes Murray has returned to more recently
concerning the relation between war, human sacrifice, and significance and meaning. The burning man offers a ghostly voice
which, when first met with, advocates a return to the kinds of
blood ritual which had formed an original religious focus in the
land. As he tells Reeby, who has been drummed out of university
for a violent dispute he has had with a group of feminist activists,

> Fellows of your caste have been withholding blood, friend.
> The women turn savage when men will not give blood ...
> It was all resolved once: this is My Body, My Blood,
> It's coming unsolved now. (BSF, 9)

Contemporary intellectualism, claims this spirit, is destructive
of rituals binding men to the other half of their nature. The lack

of real war, such as Clarrie has fought in, leads to a turning inward of aggression by both sexes. Hence the origin of the 'sex war', which centres upon Reeby, but which runs throughout the text.

Such mingled Christian and Aboriginal blood theology is then examined across the narrative, and supplies one of its most disturbing central symbols, when the radical feminist Noeline Kampff reprises the university spat Reeby had involved himself in by tipping a bucket of beef blood over him.[1] But that theology is also central to the redemption Forbutt undergoes at the end of the book when, escaped from the scene of Reeby's shooting, he enters the forest and undergoes an Aboriginal ritual: 'They take out the fatty knife and the ghastly small knife / and begin to cut' (62).

These disturbing but ordering cultural and spiritual elements in the book are, however, both countered and informed by Murray's most sustained poetic attack on the disintegrative metaphysical and political elements in near-contemporary Australian society. Whilst the tone of the writing is very much taken from the joyfully subversive act of the boys, with their 'gift of laughing at deadly things', there is much also which offers a more serious and radical critique of the forces in society opposing them. Forbutt's father is a rich liberal politician who mutters platitudes about the poor, is easily able to pay for Clarrie's body's removal to his home, but refuses to. He hangs out with Noeline, a radical feminist and abortionist, who leaves him because of his ineffectuality late in the book, but who ends up terribly disfigured when boiling water is thrown in her face in a misguided act of revenge by Reeby's girlfriend after he has been killed. This is the most disturbing moment in the book – Murray's deeply Catholic belief in the right to life becomes troublingly interconnected with Reeby's hatred for the feminist argument. However, in terms of the narrative, the maiming is impelled by huge grief.

Elsewhere, the governmental controls and regulations imposed on the local farming community through the milk and meat quota system are seen to be undermining the very way of life on the farm, which had always supported the rural poor (41, 43). That regulation in the end brings about Reeby's death, since it is whilst running illegal beef to the city that the boys encounter the policemen. This kind of immediate circumstance gains a universal aspect, as when the burning man says that the 'archaic trades are dying / all over the world' (18). But, more particularly, the feeling that traditional ways of working the land are under threat provides the essence of the vision afforded to Forbutt by his Aboriginal guides at the work's climax:

> All the new time, we've denied [the land] our culmination …
> her human life isn't in government, it is in holdings
> of literal and spiritual farming …
> or else it's in platoons, reminiscent, cheerful, deadly
>   dangerous. (65)

We are back in the realm of 'husbandry' familiar in Murray from 'Laconics: the Forty Acres' on. The sense is, as the next sonnet shows, that this kind of vision of 'the great land' is under threat even within Aboriginal culture. As the narrating voice says of the picnic Forbutt has with his estranged father and Noeline, the image the book presents is 'of a nation torn apart: / three figures around good food, averted from each other' (47). In contrast, what the book advocates is a re-centring around the native and the local. Forbutt's grief for Clarrie teaches him that

> the world is provisional, complete at every moment,
> that the centre is the First Real World. My parents'. Then
>   mine.

> That away from the centre are the losses, the stands, the
>   arrangements. (12)

In a counter-assertion to Yeats's apocalyptic vision of the fate of the modern world, we are told here that 'Only the centre holds', a thought of Forbutt's as he drifts into sleep. And yet his own 'arrangements' are fractured, since his parents' break-up and the subsequent distance from his father impel many of the arguments over meaning in the verse novel.

At its own centre, though, is the figure of Clarrie, who both sets the narrative going and provides something of its symbolic focus. As a soldier of World War I, he stands in for the 'platoons' seen as integral to the Australian way of life in Forbutt's Aboriginal vision. His is an early twentieth-century form of maleness and closeness to blood rites, which are under threat in modern society, as Murray sees it. Those rites have been replaced, as that embodiment of country values and centre of the book's network of communication, the postmistress Beryl Murchison, says, by the 'sex war'. Forbutt's father consistently holds the view that the Anzac action was either meaningless ('warfare') or grist to his blithely complacent nationalist-separatist mill: *'fighting England: / that is the secret of the First AIF, you know'* (2). At the heart of the book, therefore, is a clash of readings: a dismissal or shallow appropriation of the more authentic past by the liberal chic of the 1960s and 1970s, and a paradoxical reverence for it from the 'boys' themselves, who are both drifters in the tradition of Clarrie. In the ceremonial of the Common Dish, when, in the hallucinatory moments of the Aboriginal rite, Forbutt eats and in doing so reconnects himself with the past and the dead, it is Clarrie who offers him the 'great pan'. 'The taste suggests the holiest thing in the universe / is a poor family at their dinner. It is that dinner' (67). Yet Forbutt is also being rewarded for his own act of bravery in defying convention with regard to the funeral:

> *Do a kind act, in our code,*
> *like the one you did*
> *and the dead will speak to you*
> *in your time of need.* (68)

One of the primary things of which the liberal intelligensia is being accused is a deafness to those voices through the petty accusation that such as Clarrie were part of *'the Old Digger syndrome, the war-mongers'* (49).

Contrary to such claims, Murray seems to be calling for a true recognition of the place of such men in Australian history, since they established a code of honour and honesty that has been lost, however temporarily. As the romantic nationalist historian Manning Clark has seen it, the tragic Anzac action in Turkey paradoxically acquired for Australians 'a sacred site. The Anzacs were transfigured into folk heroes.'[2] That historically founded religious ideal resonates more fully within *The Boys* than before in Murray, although it had been often present earlier. What is striking once again is that his resulting sense of the spiritual involves both the Aboriginal and the Christian, a sense of a shared vision of humanity between the rural poor and the original possessors of the land. Although it offers a consistent view of the century's history in Australia, however, the tone of the work is necessarily inconsistent and uneven, its politics keenly felt but often coming over as intemperate and (in the worst sense) reactionary. The Aboriginal ritual, heavily dependent as it must be upon scholarly sources acknowledged at the start of the book, seems contrived, too predictable a narrative solution in some ways to the political and cultural dilemmas starkly sketched elsewhere.

As a result, Murray's continued refusal to reprint material from the work seems right. Whilst the book received a good deal of praise in Australia (many saw it as the culmination of his work to date, as becomes clear in the 'Critical Overview' below), others were troubled by some of its elements. The work now reads as a strong reaction against the kinds of decentring and disentangling of traditions Murray perceived around Vietnam amongst both the pro-American government and the protest movement, which also took its form from American culture. The complex, but ultimately unqualified, nature of the culminating ritual recalls those calls for attention to Australia's own central rites in work of the early 1970s such as 'A Helicopter View of Terrestrial Stars'. Furthermore, in the maiming of Noeline there lurks the dislike and distrust of threatening women which Murray has more recently been able to confront in himself in poems like 'Rock Music' from *Subhuman Redneck Poems*, and in the memoir *Killing the Black Dog*, where he narrates his own persecution in the school playground by girls because of his fatness. As such, this verse novel therefore seems unintegrated where it most aims to be centred.

The People's Otherworld, Murray's collection of lyrics published in 1983, took up the issue of the religious and the metaphysical in a manner which proved more wholly successful than the staged recourse to Aboriginal ritual at the end of *The Boys Who Stole the Funeral*. It is also the first collection which he dedicated 'To the Glory of God', a practice in which he has continued down to the present day. The book again shows Murray's intimate closeness with the rural poor amongst whom he was raised as being at the heart of his writing and of his sense of further possibilities, both spiritual and poetic. Yet, at the emotional centre of this work, is the sequence which gives it its title, 'Three Poems in Memory of My Mother, Miriam Murray née Arnall', a wrenchingly moving work which condenses all of the sense of injustice suffered by his people elsewhere. Miriam Murray died as the result of a miscarriage subsequently brought about by the forceps ('The Steel') which had earlier been used to bring Murray himself into the world when an overworked hospital was having to cope with several births at once. As a result of this miscarriage, the poet became an only child without a mother. However, as the longer final poem here sees it, the death was at least partly caused by social and class neglect. When help was called for, the local doctor had refused to issue the necessary orders for an ambulance to rush Murray's mother to hospital. The Murray car was broken down, and so a local teacher's car had to be used, causing a delay the poet clearly considers fatal. In the apportioning of blame, the doctor comes increasingly to the fore:

> Perhaps we wrong you,
> make a scapegoat of you;
> perhaps there was no stain
> of class in your decision,
>
> no view that two framed degrees
> outweighed a dairy. (190)

And yet, whatever the speculation here, or the forgiveness which Murray has latterly felt towards him, the doctor was driven from his practice and the town as a result of his supposed neglect ('did you think of the word *Clan?* / It is an antique / concept. But not wholly romantic' – a recourse to the Gaelic familial theme again).

What this tragic event seems to have given Murray was an early maturity ('For a long time, my father / himself became a baby') and the perception of his father's weakness, which was to seek justice for the wrongs done to him. His father also had to pay his own father rent for the shack the family lived in, rent Murray obviously feels was outrageous, given the way his father worked the family land, and failed to inherit the farm after Murray's grandfather's death – a subject touched on in the earlier 'Thinking About Aboriginal Land Rights, I Visit the Farm I Will Not Inherit'. The quest for justice seems to be a 'weakness' in Murray's eyes, because his father had failed to realize that it is not available for people like him in this world. He was 'right' to seek it, but

> The poor man's anger is a prayer
> for equities Time cannot hold
> and steel grows from our mother's grace.
> Justice is the people's otherworld. (191)

As for Eliot, Auden and Slessor, time forces an erosion of value and of what we hold most dear; but, characteristically for Murray, the recognition has its origins and resonances with regard to class wrong. Taking this realization as its cue, the book as a whole seeks to discover shareable otherworlds which redress something of the social imbalance, the 'Weights' which father and mother are seen having to carry in the opening poem of this mourning sequence. That otherworld assumes here a concerted variety of forms, from poems on objects and machines which test the distance between the internal world and the external realities, to poems on dreams and dream life, on states of mind which parallel religious experience, on the enormities of the natural world in Australia, and on the discoveries of a poetic style itself suited to expressing such possibilities. The collection represents a move forward, in other words, towards establishing a more circumspect manner than that of the more immediately engaged preceding collections. Central to all of these works is the issue of perspective, an intent self-questioning as to the particular ways in which these otherworldly expressions are to be seen. 'Bent Water in the Tasmanian Highlands', which shares an expansiveness, a mimetic accumulation of rush and flow through its subclauses typical of much of the writing, ends with these questions becoming overt:

> It includes the writhing
> down in a trench, knees, bellies, the struggling, the slack
>   bleeding
> remote enough perhaps, within its close film,
> to make the observer a god; do we come here to be gods?
> or to watch an alien pouring down the slants of our
>   anomaly
> and be hypnotized to rest by it? So much detail's unlikely,
>   for hypnosis;
> it looks like brotherhood sought at a dreamer's remove
> and, in either view, laws of falling and persistence. (179)

The onward rush of this makes it a difficult writing, sometimes difficult in the sense that metaphysical poetry is necessarily difficult. The sheer welter of 'detail' represented by the water here, and elsewhere by the Australian landscape, prevents the observer from assuming a detached view. Like many of the early pioneers in this land, this speaker is over-whelmed by it. A god-like, containing view is jostled from itself by the 'struggling' echoed by the poem's syntax. It is also disturbed by the nature of the rhetoric, which moves swiftly from the brute physical to the abstract, an abstraction which finally does seem to render some truth, 'in either view, laws of falling and persistence'.

Those 'laws', of course, rediscovered in this alien land, have their own metaphysical resonance. In this seemingly original phenomenon of the 'bent water', there is to be found an inescap-able human analogy – 'knees, bellies' – which reconfirms a fall from grace, a fall which has led to labour, struggle, and persistence. The conclusion carries religious analogy within itself, and finds it sweet and immediate ('standing / on flourish, clear storeys,

translucent honey-glazed clerestories'). Yet the issue of stance
has established the complex ways in which humans read such
possibility, and how the actual can intervene in it. Typically for
Murray, 'Bent Water' finds its own paired opposite a few poems
later, where the domesticated onrush of 'Shower' offers its own
strange meeting:

> dreamy to dance in slow embrace with
> after factory-floor rock, or even to meet as Lot's abstracted
> merciful wife on a rusty ship in dog latitudes. (183)

This 'enveloping passion for Australians' discovers for the poet a
panoply of analogies, similes and metaphors which is true to the
book's otherworldly poetics, one in which every detail can elide
into another one. Both earlier and later poems of Murray's
reveal his interest in riddles. In this collection, the focus of the
whole allows for a sense that any one subject can generate many
other possibilities.

Again we see developing a different version of that democratic poetics, one consonant with the vernacular, which Murray
had asserted in the 1970s. High and low, abstract and physical,
are brought together in the otherworld of poetry in ways which
suggest the writing's own relation to that justice denied to the
poet's people. 'Satis Passio', the *ars poetica* with which the
volume concludes, declares this forthrightly:

> Most knowledge
> in our heads is poetry,
> varied crystals of detail, chosen
> by dream-interest, and poured spirally
> from version to myth, with spillage ...
> most people's poetry is now this. (220)

Once again, metaphors of water suggest the ways in which the
intimately known can establish a continuity with something
larger, and establish a stasis in the midst of flow which underpins
Murray's kinetic art ('The fine movement of art's face / before
us is a motionless traffic / between here and remote Heaven.').
And yet within this, he is again careful of the need to establish
the fullest perspective possible – 'who was the more numinous,'

we are asked at the start of the concluding stanza, 'Pharaoh or the hunted Nile heron? / ... Beauty lives easily with equities' (221). Art, therefore, offers us 'the dream-plan / of equality and justice' which is so often denied outside its limits. Its very distance from lives enables a perspective to be engaged which will establish the true balancing of its forces.

What seems particularly Australian within this aesthetic, as the collection establishes it, is the way in which Murray recognizes that there will be 'spillage' in the process of transference from one level of reality to another, from one kind of world to another. 'Detail', as it is reflected in this collection as a whole, and as we saw in particular with 'Bent Water', also offers unmanageable excess. This is signalled near the start by 'Grassfire Stanzas', which reflect on the annual problem in the outback during the dry season, where fires rage out of control ('Humans found the fire here. It is inherent. They learn, / wave after wave of them, how to touch the country ... / It's the sun that's touched') (164–5). But, more personally, it forms the basis for the witty analogies made between Murray's own physical bulk, the passage of human history and the attitude towards life to be adopted in his country. 'Quintets for Robert Morley' offers a different take upon the nation as the 'Land of Peace', that traditional view of Australia which Murray has often interrogated within both his yarns and his consciousness of the twentieth century as marked by European wars in which many Australians died. Here, 'the fat' offer their own possibility for a different world:

> Not that the lists of pugnacity are bare
> of stout fellows. Ask a Sumo.
> Warriors taunt us still, and fear us:
> in heroic war, we are apt to be the specialists
>   and the generals.
>
> But we do better in peacetime. For ourselves
> we could spare the earth. We were the first moderns
> after all, being like the Common Man
> disqualified from tragedy. (177)

The 'Quintets' reveals that Murray has learnt from the later Auden a sense that, as the English poet put it in a poem quoted by Murray in a review of his last book, in history it is 'the misfits / ... who / altered their structure and prospered' (*PT*, 29). It confirms his wariness of all forces of progress.

And yet, in this book, such generalized perceptions are carried forward to a renewed national purpose. The sense that, for someone of the poet's size, Australia might therefore form a congenial habitat is confirmed by the exuberant 'The Quality of Sprawl':

> Sprawl is the quality
> of the man who cut down his Rolls-Royce
> into a farm utility truck, and sprawl
> is what the company lacked when it made its repeated efforts
> to buy the vehicle back and repair its image. (183)

Sprawl, from the outset, then, is a carelessness about imposed values, a resistance to the world's presumption. 'It is the rococo of being your own still centre', as Murray claims in parodic inversion of T.S. Eliot's high seriousness. Yet, once again, this assertion of an integrated selfhood with which Murray's poetry has consistently resonated, is linked with the special nature of Australia itself. Sprawl provides 'An image for my country. And would that it were more so.' The sheer size of the continent allows the florid conjunction of seeming opposites, 'full-gloss murals on a council-house wall', but also a leavening human possibility, since 'Sprawl is really classless.'

As such, it might provide further ways of entering the otherworld. In two poems Murray reflects upon the ways in which the process of human history has robbed our perception of its full numinous potential. The 'First Essay on Interest' shows the ways in which intentness on the world outside ('What we have received / in the ordinary mail of the otherworld') carries us beyond ourselves, relieving us of gravity

> for a timeless moment;
> that centres where it points, and points to centring,
> that centres us where it points, and reflects our centre.

It is a form of love. The everyday shines through it
and patches of time. But it does not mingle with these. (167)

Yet a paired (and once again contrary) later poem carries, as its title suggests, a more complicated possibility, one open to history as *this* language is not, hovering as it does tonally near Eliot's abstract diction in *Four Quartets*. 'Second Essay on Interest: The Emu' considers the matter from a more burdened national perspective:

Europe's boats on their first strange shore looked humble
but, Mass over, men started renaming the creatures.
Worship turned to interest and had new features.
Now only life survives, if it's made remarkable.

Heraldic bird, our protection is a fable
made of space and neglect. We're remarkable and not;
we're the ordinary discovered on a strange planet. (203)

The jaunty tone of this allows paradoxically for its seriousness. The incongruous look of the native bird, captured in the poem's opening, opens the way for a more general sense of incongruity which offers its equivocal view of colonization, and its revelation of human self-delusion. Unlike early works on Australian fauna, like Barron Field's 'The Kangaroo', which brought an Adamic delight to their descriptions of their subjects whilst also appropriating them to a European aesthetic, Murray's interest in the emu recognizes the out-of-placeness of the colonizers, their racism, and their loss of reverence for the creatures they found themselves amongst. Instead, the inevitable interest in the bird offers again a vision of the separate nature of an Australian spirituality, through its

           brigand sovereignty
after the steady extents of god's common immortality
whose image is daylight detail, aggregate, in process yet
    plumb
to the everywhere focus of one devoid of boredom. (204)

Under this aegis, the religious is the 'remarkable', the 'incongruous', all that Australian life offers to those truly prepared to see it.

It also involves an inclusiveness towards extremely different sights and habitats, as well as a loose-limbed and various attitude to what is being perceived. The two longer sequences in the book, 'The Sydney Highrise Variations', and the oblique love poem to his wife, 'Machine Portraits with Pendent Spacemen', show Murray taking a surprisingly flexible view of modern architectural and technological advances. Surprising, since, particularly later in his career in *Dog Fox Field*, such innovations are seen as ugly and threatening the environment. Yet, particularly throughout the first sequence, in this collection we experience a full range of possible responses. At the conclusion of the first poem about the Gladesville Road Bridge, we are told that 'It feels good. It feels right. / The joy of sitting high is in our judgement' (172). By the last poem, however, with its sense of the progressive urbanization of the interior of the country as the coastal cities grow, a more negative undercurrent has already emerged:

> Six hundred glittering and genteel towns
> gathered to be urban in plein air,
> more complex in their levels than their heights
> and vibrant with modernity's strange anger. (176)

Murray's sympathy for the rural poor throughout the book here coalesces into a sense that the loss of social hierarchies within the new and modern world breeds its own restraints and repressed violence. Yet this version of 'anger' is remote from the earlier poems in the sequence, and fails ultimately to negate their tone of celebration. Poetry, 'Satis Passio' reminds us, bestows, as Murray sees it, 'like Heaven, dignity / on the inept and the ept' (220). Or, in 'Equanimity', 'Whatever its variants of meat-cuisine, worship, divorce, / human order has at heart / an equinimity' (180).

In *The People's Otherworld*, therefore, we find Murray developing his own version of an Australian aesthetics, one in which the nature of a distinctive way of seeing is to the fore. He is also drawing out a line from earlier work like 'An Absolutely Ordinary Rainbow', when establishing that, within this context, the religious bears something of the qualities of the country itself, its strangeness and unexpectedness undermining limiting and established views.

With *The Daylight Moon*, Murray took the 'quality of sprawl' (rendered here as 'The Dream of Wearing Shorts Forever'), which had characterized the separate national consciousness of his previous collection, into new areas and specifically those of narrative and history-making. The book combines at its core a series of bush narratives, including 'Inverse Ballad', 'Relics of Sandy' and 'Joker as Told', alongside poems which offer mappings of human development (but often not development as a form of progress) across the ages, including 'Physiognomy on the Savage Manning River', 'The Drugs of War', 'Roman Cage-Cups', 'At Min-Min Camp' and 'The Line'.

The poetic texture, certainly in the early part of this collection, is significantly and consistently denser than that of the previous work – long lines filled with descriptive detail giving a full sense of landscape and natural contexts. In his essay, 'Eric Rolls and the Golden Disobedience' (1982), Murray had claimed that 'Non-fiction prose ... is clearly a vital part of our whole tradition, and is now perhaps the sector of Australian literature where specifically Australian themes, tones, concerns and even identity are most freely allowed to persist' (*PT*, 163). With this 1987 collection, Murray translates those prose virtues into his own work. As 'Cumulus' puts it,

> Neither fantasy nor fear has built an eagle's nest fortress
> to top our nonfiction poetry. We've put the wild above us.
>   (226)

In other words, the high country of the Australian hinterland, its mountainous Dividing Range, proved an inaccessible habitat for those settlers who 'turned away to ochre and surf sands long ago'. And yet those heights provided the stuff of Australian legend, its nonfiction poetry, since they provided both the hide-outs for, and the mythic fascination with, bushrangers: 'Many themes attended the hibernation of Ned Kelly.' Out of this emerges a poetics of wildness, even as Murray suggests that such wildness is now unobtainable, since 'the sleepout in the dark ranges has weakened its tug'. The thematic identity of such legends remains, however, a potential resource, and Murray's nonfiction poetry now seeks to appropriate its narrative tone to his own versions of history.

What remains consistent also is his insistence that the perspectives through which this world is viewed are themselves separate and different from that often received through literature. History-making itself comes under question. As the title of the collection suggests, this is a version of the world in which there are many incongruities and disorientations. 'The Sleepout' recalls the norm in the rural tropics whereby 'Childhood sleeps in a verandah room', when 'one wall of the room was forest', 'And out there, to kindle whenever / dark found it, hung the daylight moon' (238). From such beginnings, Murray implies, many of his later overturnings of perspective followed. The paired but opposing 'Tropical Window' and 'Louvres', poems which follow 'The Sleepout' in the collection, establish both the tone and the manner of the book as a whole. 'Tropical Window' sets the contrast between the beautiful coastal landscape seen through the 'long bright window', and the air-conditioned ease of three people looking upon it:

> Not coated glass but simple indoor contrast
> has tuned the hyaline
> to a sourceless cerebral light
> and framing has made the window photo-realist,
> a style of art everybody now feels they have been
> in. And will be in again
> at any immortal democratic moment. (239)

In the subsequent 'Louvres', the tropical world is seen from a different, ruled-across, perspective, 'through a cranked or levered / weatherboarding'. But the disorienting motif continues, as 'Every building … / is at times a squadron of inside-out / helicopters, humming with rotor fans.' Yet again, however, this disjunctive world is opened at the end of the poem, where the perspective changes once more, as 'everyone comes out on platforms of command / to survey cloudy flame-trees' during the green season. During the dry season, everyone voyages into the bush,

> or as we say the Land,
> the three quarters of our continent
> set aside for mystic poetry. (240–1)

As with the view through the 'Tropical Window', therefore, the perspective opened over these Australian vistas is one imbued with a sense of timelessness and religious potential. The 'photo-realism' nonfiction acts essentially as a way of allowing for a greater sense of the possibilities within 'the Land' both for equality and inclusiveness, but also for a distinctive religiosity. As Murray had written in his reflective article 'Some Religious Stuff I Know About Australia' (1982),

> Australians of overseas ancestry … have come to the sense, which the Aborigines had before us, that after all human frenzies and efforts there remains the great land. As George Johnston wrote, nothing human has yet happened in Australia which stands out above the continent itself. (PT, 149)

In these terms, Australian 'sprawl', a feature of the land and seasons as much as the character of the people, in Murray's eyes, represents an overflowing of boundaries in which humanity cannot contain potential. In 'The Edgeless', the next poem in the tonally defining central part of the collection, the literal flood water at a farm station inspires the couple living there to have a marooned conversation about language itself:

> We have got the word and we don't understand it.
> It's like too much. – So we made up a word of our own
> as much like nothing else as possible
> and gave it to the machines. It made them grow –
> And now we can't see the limits of that word either. (241)

Human 'progress', as it is narrated both here and throughout the book, is very much a tentative, illusory thing. Humanity is consistently forced by the 'too much' of this world to improvise and fabricate a means of expression, only to find that those temporary fastnesses are in their turn flooded – something which casts light on the impulsion behind Murray's persistent changes of poetic manner from book to book. What we find Murray doing in *The Daylight Moon*, as he has not done before, is to bring this perspective into play into a consciously formulated *poetics*. Having proclaimed in its opening lines that 'Religions are poems', the human means towards individual integration and 'whole thinking', 'Poetry and Religion' then moves towards a sense of the continuingly mobile possibility of this state. God, we are told, is in the world 'as poetry / is in the poem, a law against its closure', and therefore cannot necessarily be continually present:

> Both are given, and intermittent,
> as the action of those birds – crested pigeon, rosella parrot –
> who fly with wings shut, then beating, and again shut. (267)

In the years 1986–88, Murray wrote three essays, 'Embodiment and Incarnation', 'Poems and Poesies', and 'Poemes and the Mystery of Embodiment', in which the parallels between, and 'whole thinking' achieved through, the two possibilities of poetry and religion are explored. The Aquinas lecture of 1986, 'Embodiment and Incarnation', particularly spells out the ambition for poetry Murray was adhering to in the mid-1980s. He consistently claims that 'the poetic experience' is not confined to verse; 'it can arise from properly tuned prose, too':

> It is itself a quietly perpetual thing, this ordinary ecstasy
> … Each time we return, the poem is the same, and yet
> fresh intimations of significance are likely to arise from it.
> It is, as St Thomas said, *radiant*. (259)

Poetry, like religion, in other words, manifests a formal incarnation which in its turn has bodily effects, orchestrating the breath of its speaker, and offering what Murray calls a 'transposition of natural sensations into words' (*PT*, 264). In these essays and in the poetry throughout this decade, Murray is foregrounding the potential which had come into his life with his conversion to Catholicism in the early 1960s. Yet, at the same time, in the poetry which touches upon these parallels, we find a fully developed sense of the rarity of such radiance, of the intermittent nature of such complete embodiment. 'Infra Red', which considers astronomical discoveries about dark stars made by its dedicatee, Fred Hoyle, sees even light and radiance itself as only partially revealing, since 'Most of the real … / is obscurely reflective' (punningly, yet, due to the new science, truthfully). As a result, Murray offers his own alternative to traditional metaphors of revelation and illumination:

> Presence perhaps, and the inference of presence,
> not light, should found a more complete astronomy.

> It will draw in absence, too:
> the pain-years between a love and its fulfillment,
> the intricate spiral space of suppressed tradition. (266)

Poetry, like religion, can itself only operate in the 'real', in 'family', and so by 'inference'. As a later poem in the collection, 'The Man with the Hoe', suggests, such 'inference' is continually put into question by recent technologies ('Who could trust a God of love, now we have seen // the love that ignites stars, and ourselves possess such ignition?') (278). Yet the beautiful metaphor of sporadic buoyancy which he finds at the end of 'Poetry and Religion' in the beating of indigenous birds' wings, the slowing of time achieved there and in the universal envisioning of 'Infra Red', establish counter-strengths to such questioning. Indeed, as 'Poetry and Religion' has it, such questioning of all authorial voices ('Now why did the poet do that?') must continue as a strengthening aspect of religious possibility. The 1986 lecture 'Embodiment and Incarnation' had meditated upon the issue of religious conscience, and discovered a shared quality between conscience and art, 'an ability to be instantaneously and convincingly there … a total resistance to untruth' (PT, 267). The poems focused upon the religious resonances of art, both in their questions and in their beautifully assured freedoms, offer an active model of such conscience.

Other 'nonfiction poems' in The Daylight Moon establish their 'inference' through different means, deriving an energy and force from the 'intricate spiral space of suppressed tradition'

which Murray lists among the hoped-for temporary absences of
'Infra Red'. His narrative histories in these works act to redeem
those lives which exist beyond the bounds of the known and
written. 'Fastness' seems widely emblematic here, dramatizing
the reflective voice of the poet himself as he tries to represent an
incident during the draft for World War I, when some brothers
from the country managed to escape service through something
they said to their sergeant major. This act represents a defiance
of authority and a dubious resistance to the pressure of the times
(as a result, the brothers missed, we are told, 'their legendary /
Anzac chance'), which clearly appeals to the poet. Yet, since he
does not know their words of defiance, the nature of the defiance
eludes him:

> Since beyond the exact words, I need
> the gesture with which they were said,
> the horizons and hill air that shaped them …
>
> I will only have history, lacking these,
> not the words as they have to be
> spoken out, in such moments. (250)

What resolves the issue of the inexpressibility of such stories is
Murray's own alertness to the background behind the brothers'
plight, his ability to 'remember … the angel / poverty wrestles
with', and his sharing of parallel circumstances to those which
motivated the brothers' rejection of authority at the first slight –
'I need only / sit on this rusty bedstead, on a known / vanished
sleepout verandah and reflect.' Such intimacies are themselves a
resistance to 'history' as offered in authorized versions, and
continue for Murray to shadow them. Staying overnight 'At
Min-Min Camp' on 'a verandah / that had lost its house' – a
further incongruity of location, and location of incongruity –
Murray ruminates that

> It was a lingering house. Millions had lived there
> on their way to the modern world. Now they longed for
>   and feared it.
> It had been the last house, and the first. (260)

Such inferences in these poems suggest that history itself can only operate through a form of embodiment, and that words should not be found for what is not intimately known. 'Physiognomy on the Savage Manning River' moves from description of the landscape to reflection on the life of its first, cruel landholder, Isabella Kelly, and her brutality towards the convicts forced to labour for her. 'Walking on that early shore in our bodies' becomes, in other words, 'perhaps the only uncowardly way to do history' (233). In the 'Preface' to the sequence which is gathered in the *Collected Poems* as 'The Idyll Wheel', but which was originally an ungrouped scattering of poems across *The Daylight Moon* and the following *Dog Fox Field* (1990), Murray suggests that it is only through a particularity of detail in rendering such subjects that poetry can elude the patronising voices of the metropolis.

The sequence, which offers a poem for each month of the year April 1986–87, 'to be real ... had to be particular // since this wasn't to be a cyclic calendar / of miniature peasantry as for a proprietor.' The known, the experienced, validates the celebration of seasons once Murray had returned to his own 'last house, and the first' at his native Bunyah in 1986. Once again, he is therefore sensitively cognizant of the limits to his own proprietorship, the ways in which this last and first place in its turn eludes him:

> No one can own all Bunyah. Names shouted over oil-lamps
> cling to their paddocks. Bees and dingos tax the cattlelamps.

> As forefather Hesiod may have learned too, by this time,
> Things don't recur precisely, on the sacred earth: they
>   rhyme. (285)

The precursor Murray had looked to in his dispute with Peter Porter over the true home of poetry, therefore, is himself seen to have been perhaps presumptious in overdefining the cycle of work and days. Time itself allows for particularity and difference within seeming continuities. Therefore, Murray infers, only time opens the space within itself for the timeless, if fragile, consonances of poetry. As the poem for August, 'Forty Acre Ethno', has it,

Here, where thin is *poor*, and fat is *condition*,
'homely' is praise and warmth, spoken gratefully.
Its opposite lurks outside in dark blowing rain.

The family context offers, as 'Physiognomy on the Savage Manning River' had put it, 'some protection from history', but 'here' also 'Our children dog the foot- / steps of their grandfather, learning their ancient culture' (294–5).

A similar culture is celebrated in other poems. 'Roman Cage-Cups' seeks to hold up literally these intricate creations in glass. Nothing, Murray claims, has subsequently matched 'their handiwork / for gentleness, or edge'. The cups provide him with another parable for the alternative histories he is attentive to throughout the book. Although 'Plebs and immigrants fashioned them, punters / who ate tavern-fried pike and talked Vulgate', their endurance despite their vulnerability offers a message beyond that of standard world culture:

Some ... have survived complete and unchipped
a sesquimillennium longer than the trumpets (allude,
allude) of the arena. Rome's very hardest rock. (255–6)

Murray's view of the classical is remote from earlier emphases in Australian poetry upon mythology and refinement, by writers such as A.D. Hope. The jaunty tone of these lines almost serves as a defence against potential metropolitan carpers. It engages the possibility of allusion in all of this whilst at the same time dismissing it. The cage-cups start to take on the quality which Murray had two years earlier, in his glossy chronicle of the Australian seasons and celebrations, *The Australian Year*, found in the dry hinterland of the continent, 'a place of simplicity, subtlety and clear connections', where the simplest thing has its story and can be emblematic'.[3] They join with subjects in other poems, such as 'The Megaethon: 1850, 1906–29' – a poem about the attempted 'walking' of a steam engine from Sydney to the Hunter Valley, and the engine's subsequent reincarnations – and 'Max Fabre's Yachts', in which a seemingly eccentric local inventiveness receives a fulsome celebration.

Such 'connections' between the local and the narrative, then, lead this volume, like the earlier ones, to celebrate the bushrangers of the past, since, as one poem doing this, 'At Thunderbolt's Grave in Uralla', says, 'Now society doesn't value individuals / enough for human sacrifice' (265). These connections also impel the outraged mockery of 'The Australia Card' (one of only two poems from this book not to be included in the *Collected Poems*), a poem which derides the proposed introduction of identity cards at the time:

> What would proud Ben Hall say? Or the digs who gave
>   their all, say?
> Would they reckon that the bronze had turned to lard?
> Or merely sigh that failure
> was the first rhyme for Australia,
> and there'll soon be no Australia? Just the slick Australia
>   Card. (*DM*, 75)

The individualism which has been consistently sought and lauded in Murray's work is once more turned against the perceived totalitarian bureaucracy of the contemporary state, where the values of the past are laid to waste.

The long sequence which concluded the originally published volume, 'Aspects of Language and War on the Gloucester Road', however, itself responds to that effort of history-making through storytelling which the rest of the book thrived upon. 'Why does so much of our culture work through yarns,' the speaker here asks, 'yarns / equivalent to the national talent for cartoons?'

> It is an old war brought from Europe
> by those who also brought poverty and landscape.
> They had old scores to settle, even with themselves.
>   Tradition
> is also repeating oneself, expecting inattention,
> singing dumb, expecting scorn. Or sly mispronounciation
> out of loyalty to the dead: *You boiling them bikinis*
> *in that Vichy sauce?* We are the wrong people risen
> – forerunners in that of nearly everyone –
> but we rose early, on the small farms, and were family.

A hard yarn twangs the tension
and fires its broad arrow out of a grim space
of Old Australian smells: toejam, tomato juice,
semen and dead singlets the solitary have called peace
but which is really an unsurrendered trench. Really prison.
   It is a reminder all stories are of war.
   Peace, and the proof of peace, is the verandah
   absent from some of the newer houses here.
   It is also a slight distance. (283)

Instead of furthering the myth of Australia as the 'Land of
Peace', a myth examined from *The Weatherboard Cathedral* on,
this ambulatory mini-epic returns upon some of the national
presumptions which have often underpinned the poetry's own
methods. The myth of Australian masculinity presented in the
'hard yarns' is here perceived as delusory; its separatism and
purported difference merely a bad odour. In this New World,
the links back to war-torn Europe, with its Homeric literary
tradition, remain unbroken and claustrophobically prison-like.
Once again, the speaker of this poem is left to celebrate the small
virtues of 'peace' on verandahs – already becoming a thing of the
past – and 'family', in contradistinction to the larger movements
of national history, false solidarities proclaimed by the donning
of skewed, 'quaint' accents.

'Aspects of Language and War on the Gloucester Road' is a
complex poem which follows the speaker on a journey towards
Gloucester station 'to collect my urban eldest from the train'.
This movement gives him a 'slight distance' from us. And yet
Gloucester Road is also 'a road cut through time', one along
which the speaker recollects inhabitants of the area past and
present, and weaves his own yarns about them. The firm sense is
that, through this process, there is something therapeutic to be
gained, since 'In the hardest real trouble of my life / I called this
Gloucester road to mind' (279). As in earlier Murray sequences
like 'Walking to the Cattle Place', this is as much a mental
journey as it is a physical one, and its *poetic* implication is
established from the outset, when we are told that the road has
been 'cut'

by eight-year-old men droving cattle,
by wheels parallel as printed rhyme
over rhythms of hill shale and tussocks. (279)

The journey encompasses victories over oppression, as in the tale of Murray's father outfacing a brutal teacher, descriptions of local religious practices, and explications of local etymologies ('Bunyah, meaning bark / for shelters, or firelighters' candlebark / blown on in a *gugri* house, a word / … that is still heard'). Such passages establish not just the local historical connections, but also continuing connections between the current circumstance and the Aboriginal habitation of the land. But images of war and violence interrupt this flow, from recollections of a wartime firing range, to Murray's wartime schooling, Hiroshima, and a widower who slaughters his twenty-four pet cats ('Sweet, for one, are the uses of barbarity').

What is perhaps most striking about the poem is the way in which its attempts to reflect upon counter-possibilities to this traumatic history seem almost themselves mistimed, appearing at the wrong points along the journey. Although the drive's purpose is about reconnection with someone who might have gone astray living in the city, the ending of the poem is unsettled and unsettling. 'What else to say of peace?' we are asked near the end – 'It is a presence / with the feeling of home, and timeless in any tense' (284). And yet this glimpse of intimate eternity occurs as the poet moves *away* from home, climbing 'over the crest / out of Bunyah'. The poem concludes with a further sense of moving on and away, into a mythologized landscape beyond the poem's parameters:

I will swoop to the valley and Gloucester Rail
where boys hand-shunted trains to load their cattle
and walk on the platform, glancing west at that country
of running creeks, the stormcloud-coloured Barrington,
the land, in lost Gaelic and Kattangal, of Barrandan.

At some point in these final paragraphs, the tense of the poem, far from being 'timeless', gets ahead of itself, looking forward beyond the poem just as the speaker at the end looks out into a further country. The potentially metaphysical aspect of this 'glance', however, is mitigated by its sense that language itself cannot achieve timelessness, but rather charts a history of abandonments. At this point, the projected present merely serves as marker of a 'lost' past, with complexly interwoven settler and Aboriginal deposits. The gloom of this lost land is captured in the awkwardly compacted 'stormcloud-coloured'. The peaceful home is not where this long poem will arrive at, unlike the earlier sequence at the end of *Poems Against Economics*. Such inconclusiveness, the quick 'glance' into further worlds from the station platform, seems predicted by the title of the poem, '*Aspects* of Language and War ...', which offers us no single and settled view.

The ending of the sequence 'The Idyll Wheel', which concludes the nearly full selection of poems from this book in the *Collected Poems*, offers a similar sense of continual journeying. Instead of concluding the seasonal cycle with a sense of completion and fertile repetition, Murray establishes a further kind of 'distance', one which marks his own refusal of the farming life. *This* long poem then ends on a rather non-committal note:

> Still, farmlets and cattle-spreads also live by touches,
> A stump burning, dam scoopings, new wire stitches
> and unstated idylls had driving to and from. (305)[4]

That lack of statement, like the lost languages at the end of the originally concluding 'Aspects', suggests a limit which the poem itself cannot reach. Poetry, like the yarns which form a seemingly distinctive vernacular national consciousness, is perpetually embroiled in a conflict between historical periods and languages, rather than able to rise effortlessly above them. As Murray had acknowledged in his radio talk in 1986 on nineteenth-century Australian poetry, 'The Narrow-Columned Middle Ground', the vernacular had itself been under threat and 'dismissed as anachronistic' after the emergence of a more literary poetry in the country in the 1920s. As such, his own project is to recoup the missed potential he discovers in the essay:

a colloquial, middle-voiced poetry that catches a great deal of ordinary human experience and shares it in an unfussed way with a broad range of people. (*PT*, 232)[5]

He claims in the talk that, particularly as it had figured in local newspapers, such poetry offered the intriguing suggestion that Australian literary writing had once been strikingly of-the-moment, a modern writing preceding (and avoiding the hierarchical dangers of) modernism. But his own poetry in the latter part of the 1980s presented a more complex picture. The movement of the poetic lines represents a perpetual shuttling 'to and from'; the 'intermittent' nature of the poem's revelations, either about Arcadia or the religious, does not lead it to unmediated expressiveness. Rather, this narrative journeying along local roads evokes competing histories and claims for possession of the landscape, and, related to this, a sense of the necessarily contingent and provisional nature of the writing which corresponds to the landscape's particular 'rhythms'.

Dog Fox Field consolidated many of the preoccupations which had arisen in *The Daylight Moon*. Although usually eschewing many of the formal aspects of the earlier collection, the dense paragraphing and extended hexameter lines particularly of the opening 'nonfiction poetry', *Dog Fox Field* offers an extension of the idea of the temporariness and unfixity of realities in this context. It also reveals a more intense concentration on the acts of poetry itself, and makes more complex Murray's earlier ideas about poetry's function within history. Just as 'Aspects of Language and War on the Gloucester Road' had alerted us to *poetic*, as well as to historical and national experiences, poems like 'The Pole Barns', 'Glaze', 'From the Other Hemisphere', 'The International Terminal', 'Three Last Stanzas' and 'Words of the Glassblowers' all advertise themselves as offering analogies for the act of poetic creation alone. We are also offered several historical narratives about strange but, in Murray's view, pivotal moments in European history in 'The 1812 Overture at Topkapi Saray', 'The Lieutenant of Horse Artillery' and 'Major Sparrfelt's Trajectory', and the by now familiar rapid-fire history-making in poems like 'High Sugar', and yarns of local inventiveness like 'The Tube'. Yet the collection's predominating note seems very much to be about the necessary nature of poetry itself when set to capture the transitiveness of the world.

This note is struck from the outset, with the opening poem's narrative of the removal of a 'small timber city', Clermont, to higher ground after a disastrous flood. As buildings and streets are shifted, 'Relativities / interchanged our world like a chess game'. But, ultimately, such confusing rearrangements are seen to be apposite, given the nature of the context in which they are occurring:

> What was town, what was country stayed elusive
> as we saw it always does, in the bush,
> what is waste, what is space, what is land. (307)

In a situation where all borders are blurred, the overturning of the known world, which had seemed particular to 'my generation', takes on a wider if strange normality. The seeming one-offness of the narrated historical event itself blurs into that larger, undefined and undefining context. As a later poem in the collection about fruitless journeying, 'The Assimilation of Background', concludes, 'on that bare, crusted country / background and foreground had merged' (337).

Given this, it is impossible to establish a steady perspective from which to view the surrounding reality. In writing of Eric Rolls's *A Million Wild Acres*, Murray had noted how the style of the writing and the actual shaping of the book amounted to a distinctive perspective upon its historical material. He recalls being struck 'by the almost pointillist way in which he writes history':

> The book has historical sequence, and is arranged in chapters, but its logic is really accretive, made up of strings of vivid, minute fact which often curl around in intricate knottings of digression. ... In contradistinction to most European art ... there is little sense of foreground and background. ... Through a fusion of vernacular elements with fine-grained natural observation, and a constant movement of back-reference, he breaks through sequen-

tial time not to timelessness but to a sort of enlarged
spiritual present in which no life is suppressed. (*PT*, 175–6)[6]

We have already seen such a metaphysical syntax, one in which
each detail is separate but added to the cumulative force of the
whole, in 'non-fiction' poems like 'Bent Water in the Tasmanian
Highlands'. Here, as Rolls had done in describing the forests of
Australia, Murray seeks local features which might offer
analogies to the similar national poetics he is anxious to construct.

'The Pole Barns', which I take to be emblematic of those
poems seeking analogies for their own processes, simultan-
eously discovers once more both a sense of original craft and
contemporary debilitation. 'The sound of rain on bark roofing,'
we are told, is 'millennia older than walls / but it was still the
heart of storytelling.' Now, however, many of the barns, local
'ships of conquest', have become broken and 'roofless, bare
stanzas of timber / with chars in the text' (317). Like 'Words of
the Glassblowers', with its concluding transposition of musicality
('*Sand, sauce-bottle, hourglass – we melt them into one thing: /
that old Egyptian syrup, that tightens as we teach it to sing*'),
we are alerted to the antiquity of craft's ability to transform and
elevate reality (335). These are crafts often practised in uninspir-
ing conditions, such as 'a tacky glass-foundry yard'. But they
supply a way of shaping the local world which, Murray infers,
has continuing relevance beyond the location and moment of its
origin. As the parable of creativity, or 'knack', offered in 'From
the Other Hemisphere', observes,

> It's only the left mind
> says before you die
> you and all you love
> will be obsolete –
> our right mind, that shaped
> this poem, paper, type-face,
> has powerful if wordless
> arguments against it. (321)

Murray's essay 'Poemes and the Mystery of Embodiment'
(1988) had paid particular attention to those studies in the

pathology of perception for which this poem provides a gloss, arguing instead for magical vision through the unconscious, and a 'balanced examination of the wordless and somatic dimensions of the world-views that people actually hold'. His envy of the 'non-verbal art forms such as music and painting and ballet,' which 'retain and enrich their own special traditions of the bodily dimension', underwrites the analogy-forming manner of *Dog Fox Field*, where objects and other forms of the made stand in for, and therefore allow, reflection on the poetic craft itself (*PT*, 361).

The title-poem of the collection transposes and sympathizes with these inarticulate forces, discovering Nazism in the way in which society has treated those who did not conform to its supposedly enlightened rationality. Taking as its starting point the fact that the Nazis had proposed as a test for 'feeble-mindedness' the ability to make up a sentence using the words 'dog', 'fox' and 'field', the poem charts the plight of those so branded:

> They then had to thump and cry in the vans
> that ran while stopped in Dog Fox Field.

> Our sentries, whose holocaust does not end,
> they show us when we cross into Dog Fox Field. (332)

Taken as it stands, this might seem a suggestion founded upon deep paranoia. But then Murray, as witnessed from early on (the founding sequence in *Lunch and Counter Lunch*), has a deep antipathy for 'The Police' in whatever form. *Dog Fox Field* is again alert to the ways in which a seemingly enlightened version of historical progress masks oppression and slavery. 'High Sugar' recognizes that it was with the switch from the use of honey, which had provided the classical and early Christian worlds with sweetness, to sugar that 'millions of people / were shipped from their lives.' From this change, according to Murray, emerged continuing war ('frigates'), false fashion ('perukes'), 'human races / and the liberal mind' (335). The brutal trans-position of peoples, in other words, led, in his view, to a sense of differentiation between races, thence to racism, and so to the kinds of liberal consciousness which produce uncomprehending, knee-jerk condemnations.

Murray is, of course, knowingly treading on dangerous political ground here, offering a challenge to received opinion about the enlightened necessity of liberalism which the poetry he went on to write in the 1990s would increasingly take up. But his sense that at the root of supposed civilized values lies suppression has in itself a compelling political force throughout this collection. 'The Tin Wash Dish' provides one of the most moving works of sympathy for the poor he grew up amongst that Murray has written, to be compared with 'The Holy Show' from *Conscious and Verbal* (1999). In the earlier poem, 'Lank poverty, dank poverty', with its 'burning shames', is inescapable, whatever the possibilities for escaping from it provided by the modern world:

> Shave with toilet soap, run to flesh,
> astound the nation, rule the army,
> still you wait for the day you'll be sent back
> where books or toys on the floor are rubbish
> and no one's allowed to come and play
> because home calls itself a shack. (313)

This offers one of the frankest admissions that, whatever the achievements and success of his own craft, Murray's writing continues itself to be shadowed and haunted by similar 'shame'. Such an awareness casts a rueful light over the succeeding poem in the book, 'The Inverse Transports', where those who have obtained riches in the modern Australian state, the city *nouveaux riches* who are increasingly buying up retirement tracts of land in the country, are increasingly seen to be living behind the bars, now for security, which had formally imprisoned their transported ancestors.

'The Inverse Transports' offers also Murray's first writing out in verse of an idea which was being developed in the essays of the late 1980s, and which represents a further extension of his attention to the poetic and the somatic sides of human consciousness:

Has the nation been a poem or an accident?
And which should it be? America, and the Soviets
and the First and Third Reich were poems.
Two others, quite different, have been Rome's.
We've been through some bloody British stanzas
and some local stanzas where 'pelf'
was the rhyme for 'self' – and some about police. (314)

This establishes an inferred distinction between those forms of human creativity through history which have led to imperialist absolutism, and those, such as the one in which we read these lines, in which an individual consciousness governs a form of achieved expression. It is a distinction which informs the politics of much of Murray's subsequent work, but which also articulates the angle he had taken on both his nation's and other histories from the outset. The reappearance of bars on windows in Australia for such seemingly different – although related – reasons of enclosure offers a rebuttal, for Murray, of the notion of progress encouraged by Enlightenment thought.

Throughout these years of his career and subsequently, Murray was particularly preoccupied by the ways in which the technological advances in the modern world have thrown up their own incongruities and, more especially, threats to the global environment. 'The Billions', a poem from *Dog Fox Field* which did not make it into the *Collected Poems*, provided perhaps the most forceful expression of this. It draws upon the suggestion, being made at the time, that a solution to the problem of drought in parts of the world was to tow icebergs into regions of shortage, icebergs

towed to a desert harbour

for drink and irrigation,
stranded incongruous wet mountains
that destroy the settled scale there,
but, imported in a billion pieces

that's how the Coke world is. (*DFF*, 22)

The poem was inserted in full into the essay 'Poemes and the Mystery of Embodiment', raising it to a kind of iconic status as representative of all that Murray's poetics of integration stands against. The disruption and fragmentation imagined in iceberg importation set the poet against the forces of international capitalism, but also once more – as in his Jindyworobak allegiances – make him the advocate of an eco-political cause which sustains deep and established connections with the land. He ends by finding it 'strange' that, in the 'Surface Paradise' of Enlightenment thought, 'wanting to believe / humans could fully awaken / should take away the land.' The advocacy of somatic consciousness emerges as a resistance to those forces which, unlike the benign incongruities of the collection's opening poem, 'The Transposition of Clermont', would seek to alter ecosystems and to remove (as was also the case in the slavery narrative 'High Sugar') the people from their proper place.

Another poem which does not reappear in *Collected Poems*, 'In Murray's Dictionary', seeks to resurrect, or at least draw our attention to, the word *aplace*, which 'lasted from Gower to the Puritans', and was 'more of a true antonym / to *away* than say *back* or *home*' (incidentally, the poet has always been proud of his family ancestor, the founder of the *Oxford English Dictionary*). The historical speculation which he builds upon this lapsing of the word from usage establishes its danger. He claims that *aplace* was 'too fixed and metaphysical'. Murray's argument is that, with the disappearance of 'locality', God also becomes remote. 'It would take extremity' to bring back what has been lost (*DFF*, 74).

Other poems in the collection reveal how complex the relations to locale have often been historically. The baroquely titled 'The 1812 Overture at Topkapi Saray', which recalls a strange moment in European history, when the Turks had to choose whether to make an alliance with Russia, or to fight alone against the potentially all-conquering Bonaparte, essentially involves a typically tangled web of relationship and origins. As the opening line reveals, religious and cultural history are laden with surprising cross-currents: 'The Rosary in Turkish, and prayers for the Sultan'. Moreover, the poem focuses not upon the sultan who is making the choice ('I was holding an exact balance,' a quotation from a letter by him runs), but upon his mother, once part of an arranged marriage, who receives news from the court whilst seated in her pavilion. She is French, and played as a child with 'our cousin / the Empress Josephine', also mentioned by the son, so suggesting that all wars have a basis in extended family. Murray's conclusion from this intricate situation is surprisingly slanted towards sexual politics, as the mother at the end

> skips with Marie-Joséphe, her poor first cousin
>
> but *poor* concerns parents only. A black manservant
> attends to each girl, as they splash filigree in the tide-edge
> and gather it, as coral and pierced shells, which the men
>   receive
> for in that age young women are free, and men are passive.
>   (320)

We find here a theme which has run through much of Murray's earlier and later poetry concerning war, a sense that men are carried along by it (as in *Fredy Neptune*), whilst women stand apart. It is further questioning, in other words, of that version of manly Australian culture which has figured also in work like 'Aspects of Language and War on the Gloucester Road'. The tone of this long poem is itself 'passive' to a certain degree, offering a kind of pastiche historical documentary, a surprising spin-off of the notion of 'nonfiction poetry', which had been signalled by the opening poem in the book, and, as we will see, will be built upon massively in the verse novel of 1998 following the fortunes of Fred.

   What starts to emerge from the confusing historical situation sketched in 'The 1812 Overture at Topkapi Saray', however, is also a sense of the unexpectedness of cultural and religious allegiance following the forced transplantation of individuals. *Dog Fox Field* concludes with an epithalamium whose closing lines acknowledge once again the issue of transience:

> May inevitable troubles
> have as little depth
> as the crossing stones on which your
> godfather now rockingly stepp'th

and may the present still be
your gift, and the future ripe fruit,
when I and (it happens) many
relatives have become absolute. (359)

In this context of celebration, the poem returns wittily upon the themes which have recurred across the book. But the poem has also offered a redemptive opposite possibility within its very method, one which recaptures many of the preoccupations with the craft earlier:

When rhymers were called from broad pleasing and made
   to impress
we sacrificed rhyme, the lovelier proof that impoverished less
as it added, and skipped, and added on over the abyss.

Love never gave up rhyme:
its utter re-casting surprises never found a kindlier mime.
   (358)

The courtliness of this offers its own resistances (the wedding feast is described in terms of a medieval banquet – more elaborately so in the original than in the version in the *Collected Poems*). Murray taps his vernacular, democratic poetic here in order to offer a contemporary stay against those incongruities, confusions and historical sufferings which had resonated throughout the rest of the book. As before in his work, marriage salves and proffers its own (albeit of-the-past, 'lovelier', 'kindlier') poetic.

Dog Fox Field is one of Murray's most outspoken collections, both about historical forces of oppression and about the role which poetry must assume in response to them. In that, it looks forward to the *Subhuman Redneck Poems* of 1996. The sense of poetic possibility, of the energies it can tap, and of the narratives and allegories it can discover, seems very much to the fore as a kind of glimpsed grace which can set itself against forces of ideological, ecological, and political destructiveness. By 1990, Murray had developed a distinctive poetics, sometimes sprawling and prose-like, but always syntactically dynamic, a poetics which drew upon the improvisational qualities he found in Australian culture. Yet, throughout the 1980s, he had also reviewed the various costs and complexities of this poetic, in which native 'yarns' are seen to result from, and depend upon, larger historical and social forces. These yarns are also surprisingly vulnerable to Coca-Cola values, the 'Surface Paradise', which are increasingly flooding and threatening the world.

5

Presences
Translations from the Natural World,
Subhuman Redneck Poems and Fredy Neptune

WITH 'Presence: Translations from the Natural World', the pivotal central sequence of *Translations from the Natural World* (1992), Murray took his continuing preoccupation with issues of embodiment and realization, the vernacular and the national, appropriateness and the True Word, into a different order of poetry. This change of perspective must be seen as at least partly historically motivated. In the preface to his collection of articles and essays, *Blocks and Tackles* (1990), Murray had signalled a change of emphasis from his recent prose and poetic preoccupations, both because 'the republic has arrived in all but name', and because he felt that the republican ideal had been hijacked, like much else, by intellectuals and erstwhile radicals of the 1960s generation. This, he felt, was already producing an exacerbated form of exclusive society in Australia, one in which the working class and the rural poor were unable to realize their own ambitions (*BT*, viii–ix).

   Translations marks, therefore, a circumvention of, as well as a continuing but oblique engagement with, these more public concerns. Through these poems, which are 'voiced' for a range of native Australian flora and fauna, Murray explores notions of creatureliness and of individuality. His scepticism about the powers of rationality and of Enlightenment history, as it had emerged in the 1980s, is realized as an attempt to give expression to that which has traditionally remained beyond articulation. It is a concerted attempt to explore a version of 'mind' which has not often risen into the daylight world of expressive consciousness, or not formally so. Whilst Murray's precursors in this attempt might be found in D.H. Lawrence, and Marianne Moore, or in some of the work of his English contemporary Ted Hughes, no writer before had sought to give such fulsome voice to the differences and similarities between other species and our own. As a result, these poems from the otherworlds of the 'Mollusc', the 'Queen Butterfly', the 'Cockspur Bush' and the 'Echidna', amongst many others, marked a surprising development in the expressive qualities of Murray's own poetry, which has continued through his subsequent collections.

A poem in the first part of *Translations*, before 'Presence' (a poem which Murray has translated from a 1945 poem by Friedrich Georg Junger), gives seeming impetus to the sequence, as well as to the different syntax and vocabulary it adopts. 'Ultima Ratio' surveys the ruins at the end of World War II, and simply sets the contrary truths involved against one another:

> They hoped to make their craze
> the lasting Plan,
> now it falls apart everywhere,
> sheet steel and span. (365)

Murray's point in putting his version of the poem here would seem to be that Nazism represented the most extreme version in the twentieth century of a 'poeme', as he would call it, an attempt to graft a whole ordered, rationalized system onto events, with inevitably brutal results. As such, the year 1945 represented a point beyond which reason thankfully could not go, an illustration of the way in which all such one-sided systems must eventually collapse in upon themselves. An implied question coming out of this is where, then, a different form of consciousness might be discovered? 'Presence', with both its local focus and its particular subject matter, provides one answer.

As Robert Crawford has excellently said, the sequence 'operates through a mixture of poems which approach their subject from the (human) outside, and poems which emanate from the (non-human) inside of their subjects.' As a result, each poem 'can be seen as an act of translation, towards or away from their reader'.¹ The impulse for each poem remains, however, essentially the same – the expression of plenitude and variety through the attempt to make present the nature of its particular subject. The poem on the seemingly least, but actually most powerful, part of life, 'Cell DNA', establishes these themes, allowing both for individuality and also freedom within it. 'I am the singular / in free fall', the poem begins, but later acknowledges that this is itself due to unique happenstance. The 'rote' which DNA would seem to dictate to life was once, it tells us, a 'miscue', 'Presence and freedom // re-wording, rebeading / strains on a strand'. In consequence, difference has entered the world, difference which goes beyond the constraints DNA would seem to be able to manage (384–5). 'Cell DNA' would seem, in expressing its own subject, concerned to bring the overriding forces in the whole sequence up against each other. The attempts to establish control and separation from the rest of creation stands over and against the sense that that separation itself depends upon 'Presence and freedom', which are not self-generated. Here is individuated 'sprawl' in extreme miniature.

What seems most remarkable about the sequence is the variety of styles Murray manages to achieve in seeking to celebrate its central embodiments. Picking up on some of the techniques learned in his earlier sustained exploration of creatureliness, 'Walking to the Cattle Place', he deploys here a range of technical vocabulary. But, more often, there is a breaking with normative terms and syntax, in order to establish our distance from the subjects, and the fact that the various creatures' 'voices' are received through the difficult process of translation. The peculiar sonnet for (or is it from?) 'Echidna' begins:

> Crumpled in a coign I was milk-tufted with my suckling
> till he prickled.
> He entered the earth pouch then
> and learned ant-ribbon,
> the gloss we put like lightening on the brimming ones. (378)

The essence of the sequence is, then, a form of defamiliarization, one in which our presumed perspectives upon the world are undermined. Murray's own perspectives here are not solely ecological or religious, it would seem, but a furtherance of his persistent historical concern for the ways in which Australia has altered ways of seeing and saying. What is interesting within this is the growing sense across the sequence that, amid its welter of brilliantly realized voices, true presence in fact resides in the unsayable, in all that lies beyond even the achieved poem's reach. The experience of Australian difference is once again cast as the unfinishable Adamic process of naming its natural abundance.

The paired poems which end the work, 'From Where We Live on Presence' and 'Possum's Nocturnal Day', draw out that feeling to its fullest. The former begins with what seems an expression of human superiority, but rapidly changes towards a different sense of expectation:

> A human is a comet streamed in language far down time;
>   no other
> living is like it. Beetlehood itself was my expression.
> It was said in fluted burnish, in jaw-tools, spanned running,
>   lidded shields. (392)

To this extent, humanity's 'comet' might seem an isolation from the world of different embodiment in which it finds itself. A mere beetle defeats that expressiveness, and offers instead a presence which is defiant of appropriation (unlike for humans, 'I remain the true word for me'). The concluding sonnet, 'Possum's Nocturnal Day', would seem to make a similar point but, as its title suggests, from an opposite side. In concluding, it suggests that the non-verbal is in fact what guarantees presence, since it represents the whole from which individuality marks a fall from grace:

> I curl up in my charcoal trunk of night
> and dream a welling pictureless encouragement
> that tides from afar but is in arrival me
> and my world, since nothing is apart enough for language.
>   (393)

The unexpectedness of the syntax of the last line carries the compact pivot upon which the sequence depends. 'Me' and 'my world' are themselves expressive of a creativity which is of the nature of presence itself. In its closing lines, Murray's sequence becomes haunted by the possibility that language itself marks humanity's fallen state. In other words, that the Manichaean loss of creatureliness/creativity is a mark of our own apartness and lack of freedom and presence. What had seemed a concertedly Adamic enterprise, giving voice for the first time to the native flora and fauna of his land as the first settlers had sought to do, despite *their* impediments, turns back towards the end upon itself. The limitation and presumption of the trope of translation, which gives the sequence its own peculiar nature, is held to the fore. Subjects are returned to their otherworld, but in ways which suggest that humans have gone astray, both from an unarticulated religious possibility, and from a fruitful representation of the New World, which the past continues to haunt. Humanity's isolation in this might, however, be taken to mirror something of Murray's own feelings, as many of the ideals he had earlier held to were being overtaken by what he sees as corrupted versions of them in contemporary Australian life.

'We make out of the quarrel with others, rhetoric, but out of the quarrel with ourselves, poetry', W.B. Yeats wrote, in the fifth section of *Anima Hominis* in 1924. Murray's work, however, has consistently disturbed these opposing categories, and in the process disturbed the easy categories by which critics have come armed to question it. This becomes remarkably clear in the case of *Subhuman Redneck Poems*, perhaps his most provocative work politically, but a collection which notably garnered him the T.S. Eliot Prize in Britain in 1996. Many of these poems challenge accepted idealisms, particularly those of Murray's long-favoured targets, the liberal intelligentsia and academics. 'The Beneficiaries', for example, notoriously asks why Western intellectuals do not 'praise Auschwitz' as they should, considering that events there finally won what they had been seeking for centuries, the 'war against God' (416). Whilst the logic of the poem's argument is undeniable, its compact urge to say the historically and politically unsayable raises larger questions about how Murray now sought to position himself with regard to his audience, both in Australia and beyond. As Jamie Grant has put it, '*Subhuman Redneck Poems* ... is designed (both book and title) to tempt those who wish the poet ill to show their intentions in public.' And yet, as Grant concludes, this design is more complicated than at it first seems, since

> The difficulty for many of Murray's enemies is the fact that he often writes poems which contain both sides of an argument, with sympathy for both. Such complexity is an obstacle to the simplifying habit of those critics who like all disputes to be in black and white.[2]

A temptation for even such sympathetic critics as Grant has been, however, to map this position onto the fact that Murray was, whilst writing these poems, ill with clinical depression, an illness which is openly talked about in 'Corniche':

> It was the victim-sickness. Adrenalin howling in my head,
> the black dog was my brain. Come to drown me in my breath
> was energy's black hole, depression, compère of the
>   predawn show
> when, returned from a pee, you stew and welter in your
>   death. (412)

And yet to see the collection and its politics as simply a manifestation of that general 'victim-sickness' is to misjudge both the tone and the nature of many of its poems. The book's very title is surely as much tease as provocation, a deliberate donning of the persona of the uneducated rural reactionary which asks us to accept a distance between what is said and any unmediated expression of a political stance of Murray's own (the redneck personality had been explored thoroughly by an American poet much admired by Murray, James Dickey, particularly in his novel and screenplay *Deliverance*). As Grant concludes, the politics of the book are extremely complex. But it is important also to note that, *despite* the adopted persona, it contains some of the most eloquent work that Murray had written to date, as 'Corniche' itself fully testifies. Such eloquence suggests that, in designing the book, Murray might have had a different aspect of Yeatsian poetics in mind, the adoption of a poetic mask which creates a distance between the words on the page, albeit often in the first person, and the expressive consciousness of the author.

Furthermore, this donning of the mask might serve an intense political purpose. Edna Longley has persuasively argued that Yeats's own theory of the mask was a response to local conditions. On the one hand, there was his need to develop an idea of a separate Irish literary consciousness, and, on the other hand, his sense that his country did not yet have a sophisticated 'critical' public able to weigh the nuances and implications of such a consciousness. As a result, the mask is 'a mediating "discipline" which might regulate such relations and enable mockery without injury to the mocker ... The mask – persona, attitude, tone ... thus becomes cognate with "extending the horizon of expectations"'.[3] From this perspective, *Subhuman Redneck Poems* looks like a further development in Murray's contemplation of his complex situation in history, as a national poet both seeking to avoid the potential cultural cringe from his British inheritance and to alert what he sees as a sometimes unsympathetic local cosmopolitan audience to individuating strains within their own background. The book returns, in other words, in a different way, to many of the preoccupations of the political work of the 1970s.[4] But it is the way in which it does so that is to the point.

In this sense, the book marks also his similar concern to Yeats's in parallel historical situations, whereby Murray seeks constantly to remake himself as poet. Once the local audience has accepted one aspect of his poetic persona, he presents them with another in order to keep them alert to the nuances of what he has to say. Having seemed, in other words, to be becoming a much more literary and pietistic poet in the late 1980s and early 1990s, a poet preoccupied by issues of embodiment and presence in their formal and religious senses, with this collection Murray reminds his audience again of the political resonances of those issues. The subhuman redneck 'speaking' in a poem like 'The

Beneficiaries' is no more Murray than Crazy Jane is Yeats. But the poems voiced by these personae raise significant emotional, intellectual, cultural and political questions which are pertinent to each poet's sense of their divided inheritance.

'A Brief History', near the start of the book, is representative of the tonal values which gather in the collection. Offering as it does an often sarcastic review of elements in Australian identity, including mateship, 'our one culture', the 'beautiful claim' of the Aborigines, the 'unspeakable Whites' and the blameless Ethnics, the poem ends by rounding on Murray's old enemy, the political class, and their recent attempts to discover a new foundation for that identity by declaring the country part of Asia:

> Australians are like most who won't read this poem
> or any, since literature turned on them
> and bodiless jargons without reverie
> scorn their loves as illusion and biology,
> compared with bloody History, the opposite of home. (406)

Murray's title for this poem is two-edged, recognizing both the necessary manner of his caustic delivery here, and the 'brief' time in which Australia, as such, has existed. This latter brevity, as he makes clear in the opening stanzas, means that the country still suffers from a post-imperial note of journalistic scorn, a scorn consonant with the violence in the country inspired by the beatings suffered by its original population. And yet this, he implies, has made his countrymen vulnerable to the kinds of abstracting, pseudo-rationalistic language suffered elsewhere in the world, a 'jargon' neglectful of people's true emotional bases and attachments. Murray's 'redneck' stance here, to that extent, acts as a deliberate counter to the 'bloody History' which now fascinates intellectuals and governments. The multinationalism of the Australian government's capitalist commitments remains a consistent target of the speaker, an object of his mockery. But the ways in which progressive (and capitalized) 'History' has been deployed to exclude many Australian people remains another.

'Green Rose Tan' is another poem that operates subtly, by initially seeming to draw us into familiar Murray territory, before suddenly questioning the complacency which we feel there:

> Poverty is still sacred. Christian
> and political candles burn before it
> for a little longer. But secretly
>
> poverty revered is poverty outlived. (407)

What seems an opening statement which accords with Murray's own politics and poetics rapidly becomes more complex, as reverence becomes an inverse snobbery, revealing the actual attitude behind the policy of cultural assimilation which has marked successive governments' characterization of Australian identity. 'The mass rise into modern dignity and comfort / was the true modern epic', as we are told later. Yet, that seeming global social-engineering success-story is leading to the conglomerate colouring of things signalled by the poem's title, both 'land's colour as seen from space / and convergent human skin colour', as Murray sees it.

This convergence, then, seems to have both inherited and contemporary impacts, leading us to neglect the 'viciously poor, our ancestors' and their successors in poverty, both in India and Africa, but also 'on the kerb in meshed-glass towns.' The declarative tone is, however, adept here at taking us through various stages of identification, all of which in their turn are rendered insufficient by the speaker's argument. 'The true modern epic' is not dismissed, as we might expect it to be; rather, the speaker's own true and offensive scorn is reserved for the belated administrators of charity to the poor, the 'deodorized descendants / of a tart-tongued womb-noticing noblesse'. The speaker clearly sees an advance in the conditions of the poor, but resents the ways in which they have been helped and the costs which have been incurred, in terms of individuality and the creation of a further Third World and national underclass. As the title of the collection implies, one of the issues to be addressed is the constitution of humanity in Australia and the modern world. In this poem a label like 'subhuman' takes on a charged political force, arguing for a fuller definition of humanity itself, and hence of charity and progress.

At the heart of this issue seems to be the sense that the values (now perceived as 'subhuman' or 'redneck' or otherwise) which the nation was founded upon have been overtaken by their own forms of pietism. As 'The Suspension of Knock', a poem which directly asks about the exact location of the country and of its peoples, puts it:

> We were the proletarian evolution
> a lot of us. We've been the future
> of many snobbish nations,
> but now the élite Revolution
> that rules unsullied by elections
> has no use for us. Our experience
> and presence, unlike theirs, are fictive
> ideological constructions. (429)

The social and university elites that Murray still feels to be the true (unelected) rulers of the country have replaced both future and past with ideology, one in which the true values of the people and democracy are ignored. However, a later poem, addressed to Murray's actual ancestor who set out from Scotland to the new colony, complicates this further. 'My Ancestress and the Secret Ballot' seems both to praise the Australian invention of the form of voting which ended gerrymandering, and lament the kinds of social welfare which subsequently arose from the consequently elected left-wing parties, who offered the poor 'the only non-murderous route to the dole'. This wry ballad in fact ends by mockingly wishing the role of settler had never befallen the poet's family, who left their own country through poverty ('wait just a century and there'll be welfare / in full') (452). Whatever the benefits of the politics such exigencies bore, Murray implies, the neglect and the violation of indigenous rights in this 'stolen Austral land' can lead to (as they have often been proclaimed to have done) no complacent acquiescence in history or sympathy for those suffering oppression.

What is most impressive, perhaps, about *Subhuman Redneck*

Poems is the ways in which it discovers those forces of violation as they begin to register themselves. The casual brutalities of the playground, 'the true curriculum of schools', are explored in 'Where Humans Can't Leave and Mustn't Complain'.[5] 'Rock Music' laments the ways in which contemporary emphases on sexuality and sex exclude the shy and the physically 'inadequate' ('Sex is a Nazi. ... / To it, everyone's subhuman / for parts of their lives. Some are all their lives.') (410). 'It Allows a Portrait in Line Scan at Fifteen' offers a deeply moving rendition of the world of autism as it is lived out by Murray's son, and of the innocent virtues he expresses ('He is equitable and kind, and only a little jealous.') (431). 'On the Present Slaughter of Feral Animals' presents a scornful attack on the shooting, supposedly for population control, of thousands of indigenous animals with high-powered rifles from the safe distance of helicopters:

> It is the hidden music of a climaxing native self-hatred
> where we edge unseeing around flyblown millions toward
> a nonviolent dreamtime where no living has been. (425)

Once again, complacency and non-questioning are the subjects of, and incitements for, this attack; Murray's interest in 'nonfiction poetry' and 'prose' has been sharpened here to enable a voice of provocation which raises important racial and national questions. As 'The Genetic Galaxy' delights in revealing, everyone embodies some mixture of racial types, and the oddness of this needs displaying as openly as possible, since it 'might stun revenge, sheer wealth of tangents / heal affinity and victimhood. ... / I'm one eighth of a musketeer, being slightly a Dumas / on my Aboriginal side' (464). Not only in Australia, in other words, is creolization a historical fact and political possibility. But that very mixing provides also a space for imaginative play and revelry. In other words, the Australian predicament and possibility provides a wry model for all modern living.

Far from seeming the result of its own victimhood to clinical depression, in other words, the political feeling of these poems often emerges from a supreme flexibility and generosity. What is revealed perhaps most sharply is the sense that the political has never been far from the surface of Murray's own first-person accounts of his experience – a fact which is hardly surprising to his sympathetic readers, to whom the collection is also clearly directed, as those most likely to be tuned into its specific and difficult tone. As the stunning elegy to the poet's father, 'The Last Hellos', ends,

> Snobs mind us off religion
> nowdays, if they can.
> Fuck thém. I wish you God. (450)

In its assertiveness about a way of life and a vision of the world, this is not tonally remote from the stroppy 'The Beneficiaries'. Yet it reveals fidelities which are unbreakable alongside social divisions which continue in their hurt.

None of which is to proclaim, perhaps, a particular power for the poetic acts which embody these provocations and fidelities. Two poems, appearing in a typically paired fashion from Murray, seem to question and explore some of the essential elements in poetry-making. In his version of Ovid, 'In Phrygia, Birthplace of Embroidery', he describes the victimhood of Midas, who has lost his faith in the gods, and as a result 'either they or their haughty absence sent him metaphor, // an ever-commencing order' (418). As a result, the world loses its reality for him, as he loses his ability to touch it ('his wife was like an aged queen, and his heir like a child.'). Conversely, 'Like Wheeling Stacked Water', the collection's subsequent poem, reveals how, in the face of extreme natural events particularly – here it is a great flood – metaphor and simile can perform a humanly hopeful task ('*Like* is unscary milder love. More can be in it.'). That propensity for likeness can then blend times and worlds, enlivening a continuing possibility: 'All this is like the past / but none of it is sad. It has never ended' (419).

In these poems which directly address poetry's potential, therefore, Murray seems concerned with those twinned issues of distance and proximity which play beneath the 'subhuman redneck' mask across the collection. Like Midas, the speaker of some of these poems can seem remote and open to mockery in the aureate smugness of his argument, but also never fails to challenge the expectation and complacent acceptances of class and social structure in the modern world. 'Modernism's not modern: it's police and despair', as 'Memories of the Height-to-Weight Ratio' – a poem which recalls Murray's enforced slimming in order to keep his job and feed his family – aggressively puts it (426). And yet, and at the same time, the speaker of these poems can express an astonishing sympathy and understanding for those local values and ways of life which challenge multinational orthodoxy. In 'The Rollover', for instance, there is a surprising lament for the eviction from their jobs and homes of those old-style bankers who had understood the needs and cash-flow rhythms of the rural poor ('It's Sydney or the cash these times.') (411). The politics of the collection, in other words, are direct and also subtle, consonant with a poetics wary of those forces of capital and convergence that threaten its true uniqueness.

The year 1998 brought the publication in book form of Murray's most ambitious work, and his second verse novel, *Fredy Neptune*. Advertizing itself, through its deployment of unrhymed eight-lined stanzas, as a modern epic in the tradition of Byron's *Don Juan*, the book relates the fortunes of its hero from the outbreak of World War I down to just beyond the mid-point of the twentieth century. And yet Murray's 250-page epic contains none of the digressiveness of Byron's work. He avoids that distancing, all-knowing narration, which would set him, as poet, apart from what Byron himself called 'my people', the characters in the poem. Whilst the central figure utters, and hears uttered, some opinions recently voiced elsewhere in Murray's writing (such as 'Sex is a Nazi'), he is not himself *placed* by any external voice in the text (*FN*, 195). Instead of the multiple authorial speculations and romantic uncertainties entertained by (and entertaining in) Byron's work, we have here a multitudinousness of narrated events, in which Fred is swept, often bewildered and bewilderingly, from one incident to the next. In this removal of an external narrative voice, as in much else, *Fredy Neptune* is an epic of Australian working-class life in the early part of the twentieth century, one which takes its manner as well as its tone from the people it tells of (Fred's name here is an ironic use of the standard Australian name for an uncultivated bloke, like Alf and Ocker).

Yet the poem is also, in a surprisingly literal and compelling way, a distillation of many of the ideas which Murray had worked through in his articles and talks of the latter part of the 1980s, particularly those about religion and embodiment. The tale is predicated upon an incident of World War I described in the version of an Armenian poem by Siamanto, which stands as the book's epigraph. The poem relates to an incident in the Second Armenian genocide, in which a group of women were ordered to dance, and then were set alight by Turkish soldiers. The incident clearly stands alongside the many mass murders which characterized the first part of the century, many of which are narrated in the book. But Fred's response to witnessing the massacre at the opening of the work is to lose his own sense of touch, as though in expiation for what has occurred. Whilst his touch comes back intermittently throughout the novel, and fully returns only at its end, the main effect of his response is to turn him into a kind of picaresque superman. He is capable of enduring amazing physical hardships without suffering, and able to perform stunning feats of strength which suit him perfectly, at several points of the novel, to a life in the circus (*Fredy Neptune* is his stage name). This gives some of the narrative a vaudeville feel, ideal for the world of early Hollywood in which Fred finds himself absorbed, as a bit-part actor, at one point. But it also makes Fred into a representation of one of his creator's key preoccupations, in the 1980s, with bodies and the mysteries of embodiment. As a response to atrocious historical events, which are conveyed for the reader in their full dreadfulness throughout, Fred is rendered into a body with no presence, for himself or in the world, in the sense that he can no longer register the environments in which he finds himself.[6]

In his essay 'Poemes and the Mystery of Embodiment' (1988), Murray had argued for the inclusion of the body in consideration of our normal somatic and imaginative lives, lives in which thinking and dreaming undergo a fusion:

> Just as our body is something of a constant, modifying the flights of our thoughts and our dreams ... fusions of thought and dream also arise from it without being called into existence by external stimuli. Just as external purposes borrow our body, its work and sweat and needs, to serve their embodiment, so it borrows from the infinite repertoire of externals to embody its happiness. ... If a poem is not embodied in art, it may well requisition other people's bodies to give it some embodiment. Don Juan's poeme did; so did Napoleon's. (*PT*, 366–7)

Murray means by 'poeme' here, as elsewhere, those ordered, rational dreamings about the 'true nature' of the world which form both ideologies and religions. As such, Hitler, Marx and Stalin are, in this view, poets. But, since their vision could find no embodiment in art, they demanded human sacrifices to bring their respective poemes to some kind of conclusion. It is only, by contrast, in the integrative space of a true poem that peaceful shapings of such visions can be brought about. What happens to Fred in this novel is itself an embodiment of this notion. He suffers under some of the major poemes of the century, and seeks to help those who are similarly threatened or afflicted. External events horrifically overwhelm and render null his internal life, and he cannot attain peace.

Such events also, in the inventive passive syntax Murray uses to get Fred to articulate his condition, lead to an inability to relate to others. On one of his ships (his itinerant life is supported by his working at sea), he reflects early on:

> No pain, no pleasure. Only a ghost of that sense
> that tells where the parts of you are, and of needs inside
> so I wouldn't disgrace myself ...
> I was having all this private life and working my watches
>   too,
> not liking to sleep in full dark because of the way
> my body, it would fade, and leave me just a self in mid-dark.
> Strange to tell that, even now. No one on earth to tell then,

a working man with other working men, ashamed of the
difference happening me. (9)

That reticence, which Murray had earlier seen as a characteristic
of Australian men, and which he felt might be established, as in
'The Mitchells', as the basis for a separate vernacular republic,
here manifests another inflection, one expressive of the truth of
affliction. To that extent, Fred's poem, the novel he speaks,
offers an antidote to the suffering he had formerly undergone.
Only at the end does he achieve the 'fusion' in himself whereby
he can truly respond to the external world in ways which allow
him to achieve fulfilment and rest from his long journeyings by
land and sea. His response to those who come to suspect his
secret is to move away out of shame or fear, and the narrative
momentum of the book is at least partly governed by this,
alongside other impulses brought about by the advent of war
and poverty.

Fred's developing sympathy is with those who have suffered,
or who are under threat of suffering, those with similar literal
disembodiments and oppressions to his own. Near the beginning
of the story, he witnesses an odd event in the Netherlands, in
which a girl's artificial arm is detached as she is being robbed:

The girl was crying, with the sleeve torn off her blouse
and I was the one nearest. I was so stupid-shy,
she was stretching out her hand, her real live hand –
and what do I do but put her wooden arm in it?
If I had got that right, everything would have been
different. (8)

The 'stupid-shyness', the inability to touch those who are
suffering similar plights to his own, is something which, across
the progress of the epic, Fred learns to overcome. He performs
saving feats of strength by, for example, lifting a car off an
accident victim or by preventing a log-roll which threatens the
life of a timber worker, but it is his growing sympathy for the
oppressed that moves him towards salvation. In the latter stages
of the book, Fred rescues Hans, an autistic child who is to be
sterilized, with his family's consent, under the Nazi sterilisation

programme, and smuggles him out of Germany – a final example
of the ways in which Murray feels that poemes which have not
become poems inflict damage upon bodies (it is also attuned
with those anxieties about emasculation in his earlier work). It is
whilst watching Hans playing tennis with himself by hitting a
ball against a store wall that Fred moves towards final and
lasting relief from his affliction:

> I sat to wait. There was a crucifix
> on the wall near me, and Jesus had his head turned hard
> to one side, as if he was watching just one player
> in Hans's tennis game; not Hans but the dark shape that kept
> returning his shots, mostly skew, so Hans had to chase them.
>
> You have to pray with a whole heart, says my inner man
>   to me,
> and you haven't got one. *Can I get one?* (254)

Fred has been told, by a mysterious hooded figure during a
visit to the Holy Sepulchre in Jerusalem during World War I,
that prayer will release him from his loss of feeling: '*Your
response to the death of our sisters is good / best of all outsiders.
If ever you can pray // with a single heart to be free of it, it will
leave you that day*' (14). The rare rhyme offers, musically, a
premonition of that consonance and integrity which comes to
Fred at the end. He arrives at health through a unique, though
surprising and problematic, understanding that it is the victims
of history who are to be forgiven by the victors, and not the
other way round. Fred is personally responsible for no deaths,
and has victimized no one. Yet, at the same time, the poem
concludes, he cannot escape the fact that he is partly what he is
because of their sufferings. So, his 'inner man' recognizes that
the path through this is by coming to a spirit of forgiveness
towards such 'others' as Aborigines and women:

> Forgive the Jews, my self said.
>
> That one felt miles steep, stone-blocked and black as iron.
> *That's really not mine, the Hitler madness* – No it's not,
>   said my self.

It isn't on your head. But it's in your languages.
So I started that forgiveness, wincing, asking it as I gave.
   (254)

Fred's recognition goes controversially against that recent
cultural and political movement towards developing greater
sympathy with the victims of history. It might partly be
explained by a trend of growing annoyance coming through a
column Murray contributed to the *Independent Monthly* from
1993 to 1996, during the time in which *Fredy Neptune* was
being written. He was increasingly impatient with the ways in
which white and British-origin Australians were being held
solely responsible, by 'brainwashing' intellectual forces in the
state, for the plight of the Aboriginal population throughout
history: 'No allowance is made, usually for the tragic unwilling-
ness of our first settlers, nor for the very different world-view
under which the continent was settled' (*WF*, 82–3). He finds the
policy of multiculturalism, which had been developing from the
time of the Whitlam Labor government in the early 1970s, an
ideological trap which was becoming more exclusive of white
single-passport holders, and also 'unreal' 'in the workaday
world where people marry across cultures and rub along with
each other whilst making a living'. Once again, the theme of
mixed, creole society stands as an ideal under which one which
would interweave, rather than subsume, divergent elements.
Forgiveness here emerges as an everyday coming together which
involves both the oppressors *and* the wretched of the earth.

   It is that concept of cross-cultural understanding and
normality which, more than anything else, seems to motivate the
forgiveness of those oppressed, and which forms the releasing
prayer for Fred. He is one of the Boettcher family from Dungog,
and it is his German origins which get him embroiled in World
War I, when he is inadvertently carried away by one of the
German warships lent to the Turks whilst his merchant ship is re-
coaling it. It is as a result of this that he witnesses the burning of
the women. The apparent rootlessness of his background,
however, is what proves throughout the novel to be his strength,
and the basis for his pacifism in a half-century almost wholly

given over to war and the fear of war. *'I can't enlist,'* he later tells members of the Remount Centre providing horses for the frontline troops in Egypt, after he has fallen amongst Australians again. *'You mean, you won't shoot Germans? – / No. And nor Australians'* (13). Fred, in other words, remains a sailor at heart if not in fact, an Odyssean traveller across the face of the earth from Australia to Europe and the United States, rather than becoming embroiled in the violent confrontations of the century. He could in a sense be seen as the embodiment of that migrancy which Salman Rushdie and Homi K. Bhabha have seen, in relation to other cultures, as inevitable in a move towards a postcolonial condition, were it not that he is part of no diaspora or forced movement of peoples.[7] 'There were no sides for me: both were mine. I'd seen them both. / Better to lie than pick one: better die than pick: and I'd died indeed / flesh-dead, alive in no-life' (17). His physical response to horrific suffering is, as he later concludes, determined by 'A way I couldn't let the world be' (251).

As his 'inner man' says at the end, he cannot exculpate himself from these events; they are part of his being and language. And yet his being of two countries underlines his difference from what the world is implicated in. During an argument with his mother, once she has moved to Germany during the rise of Hitler and married for the second time, Fred realizes that *'Split belonging's killed war, in me. / Being on any two sides spoils you for all sides'* (182). His mother, now married to a petty estate agent who gets his kicks as a Nazi sympathizer, cannot understand this (*'For right against wrong? snapped my mother. For decent against low?'*). Fred's sadness at these Nazi overtones consolidates his own perspective, and moves him towards his concept of forgiveness at the end. His mother's bitterness and sympathies are, though, partly motivated by her experiences during World War I, when Fred's father had died of the strain brought on by the hostility and violence faced by many German settlers in Australia. But Fred's 'split belonging' allows him to utter a notion matching the early conception of the country as a unique Land of Peace, claiming in the wake of World War II that

These here were my people, but too much so. Our
  Germanhood
was bleached manageable at the world's other end. (197)

Away from Europe, the racial antagonisms and imperial
ambitions are dissolved away. What characterizes Fred's awareness of this throughout the novel is his immediate rapport with
those who, like himself, are on both sides at once. While
attached to a circus as a way of surviving, he forms an innocent
rapport with Leila, who, as he does not realize, is a transvestite
('Well, a bloody fool was something I could feel. / Even her
peeing standing up') (239). Leila, too, has realized that men were
responsible for 'practically / all the horrors done in my lifetime',
and so opted out. In Cairo, during World War I, when Fred is on
the run from yet another cohort of doctors seeking to understand his condition, he runs into 'Sam Mundine the Jewish
Aboriginal / bait-layer from backblocks Queensland', who helps
him get away, and who becomes a lifelong friend (24). During
World War II, Sam is involved in getting his fellow Jews away
from Germany, despite their obvious reluctance:

> Most Jews won't listen.
> Run, from that corporal? We're Germans too. It'll return
>   top normal. –
> Aren't they really Germans, though? I asked. Are
>   blackfellers Australian?
> Sam asked me. If you're different are you the same?
> That one reached right through me. (205)

At such points, the novel involves us in the (literally) sentimental education and development of understanding of its hero.
Whilst he seems assured of his unique national and personal
position at the start, and of the potential which it opens for him
('God sees both sides'), it is only through his experience of the
'poemes' of oppression that he comes to a full knowledge of the
realities involved, and so of the need to forgive. As such, he
seems like one of the innocents, the 'holy fools' of Russian
literature, but also one who comes quickly to understand the
implications of ideologies which will later cause mass deaths –

he is aware of the threats of Nazism, for example, from the early 1930s.

At times, this can make the plotting of the book seem somewhat contrived, as though Fred's picaresque progress as a figure of early twentieth-century history must allow him to witness *all* of the century's oppressions. The long episode in the United States during the Depression, for instance, involves him in both desperate poverty, as he adopts a hobo's life of jumping the trains, and also in preventing racial violence (144 ff.). Conversely, he encounters there a weird imported version of what initially seems a Murray-like ideal of somatic unity in the figure of the aptly named Thoroblood, an Australian on the run for having cheated in business whom Fred has been forced to hunt down: 'He would talk … about / bodies and corporals, embodiment and incarnation / … about how a true poem could arise / from the body' (121–2). And yet, as the self-parody and the character's name implies, this dream hides a version of bodily purity which prefigures that of the Nazis (a danger in thinking through 'embodiment' which Murray is alert to in the essay on 'poemes'). However, chaos ensues, as the odd collection of superhumanly strong men Thoroblood has drawn together in his commune finally rebel and destroy the place.

All of this takes much narrative time, and, whilst it furthers the central theme of the novel and varies it, does not bring us much further towards understanding the historical basis of Murray's preoccupations. What such *narratively* digressive episodes confirm, however, is his very different approach to poetic form. Fred's two-sidedness and resolute scepticism about people not from his background lend him an improvisational nature. As he reflects at one point, 'We discover life, I reckon; we make it up / on the hop, as it strikes us' (33). The structure of the novel, like that of the earlier *The Boys Who Stole the Funeral*, embodies that sensibility, one settled in no one place and therefore open to all. The idiom of the novel is, therefore, the 'middle voice' that Murray had consistently celebrated in earlier Australian writing. Fred's own speaking voice is alert to social nuance and exclusion in others' speech, but is also to-the-moment and rapid in its narrative switches. After a wrestling match he surprisingly gets involved in with Lawrence of Arabia, Fred overhears the crowd commenting on him:

Quite a little performer!

they said. Where I grew up, 'performing' meant
crying in public. Or raging. Anyway chucking the emotion
    about.
But it doesn't mean that among the quality. This was the
    Sunday.
On the Thursday following, Hell broke over Palestine
and I was out flying in it. (35)

The rhythm of the work, therefore, very much follows that of Fred's narrating voice, and his own social sensitivities. Yet such encounters with the historically renowned seem also to serve an important function in deflating the whole standard notion of heroism and of history as the achievements of the great and the good, a deflation with which the choice of Fred as 'hero' here is ingrained. Even his encounter with the poet Banjo Paterson, the head of the Remount Centre, serves a similar end. Paterson, as promulgator of an attractive version of male Australian individualism on horseback, is made to reflect on his ballads in ways which recognize, in the context of modern war, their anachronistic nature ('*My poems? Of course / they may be nothing but a long farewell to the horse*') (22).

Interestingly, Murray's consistent claim in his occasional prose that the characteristic 'middle voice' of Australian poetry – one to be found in nineteenth-century newspaper verse rather than in verse such as Paterson's ballads – is modern before modernity seems most borne out in the passages where Fred's ability to improvise and adapt carries him to early Hollywood. Whilst part of his time there is typically spent in sheltering a family driven from their home by the Depression, what is also compelling is the empathy Fred finds with the actors, or those who wish to break into the movies, as with the whipcracker Tex, who asks Fred and his mates:

You boys work in movies?

He wanted to himself. He was posing for it, making himself
  up
as a story, like most of them. Not much harm in it.
Most folks preen and watch themselves sidelong,
playing themselves, the Farmer, the sacrificing Mother.
It's just I was jealous. I had to live mum, with my story,
and never let it show. When they asked did we know Tom
  Mix
and Pola Negri and the rest, I told them those were just
characters. Different actors played them, different times.
  (154)

As the title of the novel suggests, Fred's divided position,
both of the world and not of it, both German and Australian,
allows him to acknowledge the power of fantasy, and of the
ways in which the modern world – in contradistinction to its
concurrent apocalyptic destructiveness – has embraced it. As the
novel progresses, any extraordinary event is described by Fred
as 'pure Hollywood', as in the food he acquires when helping to
dismantle an American base at the end of World War II (246).
His earlier encounter with another German acting in the
modern medium of film, Marlene Dietrich, both enhances our
sense of the normality of those who have had iconic status
thrust upon them (she brings food to his apartment and cooks
for him), and deepens his sense of the double-sidedness of the
modern world itself (on first seeing her he thinks she is 'the
most beautiful woman / we ever saw in a white sharkskin man's
suit') (152). During another meeting with her, she recites
Rilke's 'The Panther' in translation (two-sidedness again), and
so offers Fred, whose physical plight she suspects and
understands, a metaphoric version of his own life ('*To him it
seems steel bars are infinite, / a thousand bars, and no more
world beyond*'), as well as of her own, a watched and idealized
image out of touch with the world.

The subtlety and self-awareness of such encounters set the
character of the central figure apart from earlier suffering
national heroes or icons such as C.J. Dennis's 'Sentimental

Bloke', the larrikin hero of a series of books published at the time of World War I, with whom he might otherwise be associated. Fred goes beyond that dated world, somewhere between 'folk balladry and popular comic theatre', which Murray has seen the Bloke as inheriting. His mixed and racy idiom carries none of the overlay of social argot which makes Murray so uneasy in the Bloke's case, fearing, as he said, that the non-standard idiom Dennis uses for his hero sets him up as a kind of stage Australian (*PT*, 281). Fred literally embodies that sense of the necessary creolization of Australian culture and nationhood which Murray has consistently argued for. But his story reveals both the difficulties and the sufferings which must truly be undergone, the history which must be escaped, in both Australia and beyond, before it becomes possible to live that situation. As such, *Fredy Neptune* represents the most complex, imaginative, and engaged rendition of Murray's meditations upon the distinctive nature of his country and of its people, one where Fred dramatically involves his readers in the fullness of the life which is opened to him by his condition. As he sardonically ends his tale, 'But there's too much in life: you can't describe it' (255).

6

Critical overview and conclusion

İF the poet Geoff Page was exaggerating a bit when, in a review in 1984 of *The People's Otherworld*, he claimed that 'the poetry of Les Murray has only just begun to receive the close critical attention which has long been its due', he was not exaggerating very much.[1] Although Murray's work, from the second collection onwards, was being printed by Australia's foremost poetry publishing house, Angus and Robertson of Sydney, and each book was being (more or less) respectfully reviewed in three or four (mainly Australian) papers and journals, the consistent sense was that Murray was being neglected. Christopher Pollnitz, in his detailed 'survey' of Murray's work to date in 1980, noted that although the poet had been actively publishing for over fifteen years by then – and despite the appearance of a study guide to the work in 1978 – there were still only two non-review articles about him, and one of those was already nine years old.[2]

This sense of neglect had been addressed several times by Murray's strongest advocates in the 1970s, when reviewing new collections. The poet Robert Gray, writing on *Ethnic Radio* two years after the book had appeared, blamed the 'depressing lack of enthusiasm' about it on the low expectations of poetry editors in Australian magazines, who allowed column after column of work by 'ambitious non-poets' to appear in the place of decent work. 'The Buladelah-Taree Holiday Song Cycle' in this collection, Gray claimed, was 'one of the two best poems ever written in this country', and stood alongside Kenneth Slessor's

'Five Bells'.³ The poet and novelist David Malouf had greeted Murray's previous book, *Lunch and Counter Lunch*, with a similarly perplexed question about the lack of 'serious' critical consideration for a collection which 'contains some of his best work to date.' Malouf's own response was perhaps more revealing than that of Gray and of other writers who put this neglect down to the cultural insufficiencies of the country:

> Les Murray's general stance, as commentators have already noted, is conservative ... Most of these poems are straight-forwardly Christian ... They are also about such unfashion-able subjects as nationhood, the need for law and order, the blood tie with land, and the manly virtues ... The book is meant to make us uncomfortable.

Whilst Malouf noted the 'flexibility' of Murray's conser-vative thought, and the confirmation in the book that he is a 'major poet', the keynote of the review was the 'way-out' nature of such work 'given the current climate'. The various attacks in the book on the university-educated elite, and its consequent recourse to 'traditional Australian values', set it outside the liberal consensus then dominating the reception of poetry in the country. Malouf was anxious to distance himself from such an elite, proclaiming that Murray's 'attitudes' were not 'worrying' since the poet was 'more caring, more human, than his antagonists'. What did concern him, though, was the new tone in these early works of the 1970s. The poems now 'have their source outside the poet: they are points in a public debate'. The tone was, as a result, 'too often preachily rhetorical and condes-cending'.⁴

Malouf's concern has formed a consistent note in the reception of Murray's work, particularly in Australia. His status as a major poet, even as the best contemporary poet from the country, goes along with a consistent feeling that the poetry has too often given way before *extrinsic* impulses and rhetorics. The 'conservative' label had been implied, even if with praise, from very early on, as in Ronald Dunlop's review of the second collection, *The Weatherboard Cathedral*. These poems, Dunlop felt, confirmed Murray as 'a poet of the outback' in the best Australian traditions – 'The poetry comes directly from his knowledge of and affection for the land and its people.'[5] When he reviewed the next collection, *Poems Against Economics*, Roger McDonald noted Murray's 'almost dietetic belief in the restorative values of a rural culture', a belief which allows the poet to gather 'poetic energy'. When Murray wandered from that culture, however, as in the poems about Vietnam, McDonald felt that he became needlessly obscure.[6] Once again, tension here was perceived between Murray's 'true' subject, the culture from which he came (regardless of whether that subject is valued by the critic or not), and the 'propagandist' Murray, one whose interest in national identity threatened the poetic virtues of his writing.

These issues came to a head with the publication of the first version of *Selected Poems: The Vernacular Republic* by Angus and Robertson in 1976. Penelope Nelson, whilst perceptively (given his later development) noting that Murray's 'central subject matter is ritual: ritual in the religious sense of something sacred and apart', also recognized a preacherly attitudinizing in the more recent work. She mounted a counter-offensive against those who saw him as merely enacting a 'retreat from contemporary realities' in writing about the countryside, but, in conclusion, was clearly worried about a further attitude this might trap him in – a 'soft primitivism' in which 'past eras and lonely places are cast in a glamorous, innocent light'.[7] Gary Catalano felt that, on the basis of the *Selected Poems*, it was true but surprising to think 'that Murray may be a better poet when his themes are closer to intimacy and love than to warfare and nationhood'. Despite his 'delight' at the more 'intimate' poems, therefore, Catalano argued that Murray's conceptual world 'is an utterly mechanical one'. Further, he cited a tension in the work which was to preoccupy later commentators, and which did indeed form a central conflict in the work, arguing that 'both his ethnocentricity and his vast range of reference hinder his attempts to encourage a sense of community. His poems are not only difficult to comprehend but also difficult to *memorise*.'[8]

These perceived strains within Murray's work and the sense
of the conflictual issues involved in reading him, inevitably
came to something of a culmination with the appearance of *The
Boys Who Stole the Funeral* (1980), the work which contained
the poet's most extreme attacks on the lack of values, as he
perceived it, in modern Australian society. However, the result,
in terms of his critical valuation within Australia, was often
unpredictable. Catalano himself found it 'the best thing Murray
has done'. He noted the centrality accorded to the woman, Beryl
Murchison, saying that her presence confirms 'the truth of its
author's declared values'. As a result, he felt that Kevin Forbutt,
the central male character, was underdelineated. Whilst he
deplored the disfigurement of Noeline Kampff, which seemed to
run counter to the Christian framing of the story, Catalano
reiterated that the verse novel was Murray's 'greatest
achievement'.[9] On the other hand, Christopher Pollnitz, who
came to the end of his comprehensive 'survey' of the poet's work
with *The Boys*, saw the disfigurement as 'offensive', confirming
Murray's adherence to the 'Old Testament ... law of retribution';
therefore, he saw the volume as a whole as 'damagingly
transitional'.[10] The novelist C.J. Koch, on the other hand, saw
the book as a 'watershed', not only in Murray's work but in the
history of Australian writing. For him, its hybrid form, operating somewhere between poetry and novel, and its central rite of
'Common Dish', offered a 'radiant' exemplification of a 'national'
possibility.[11]

Peter Porter, one of Murray's principal advocates abroad,
despite the two poets' ongoing 'dispute' over the Athenian or
Boeotian origins of poetry, typically warned foreign readers in
an article of appreciation in 1982 that 'Nobody should read *The
Boys* who has not first absorbed Murray's other poetry, since its
aggressive tone is directed at [an] Australian readership, and is
part of a long-lasting, small-print argument about value for the
forthcoming republic.' Given the inward-looking nature of its
preoccupations, however, Porter contentiously saw the book as
Murray's most 'baroque achievement', making him 'the most
accomplished and inventive poet in Australia today'. 'Baroque'

was Porter's wicked if witty way of circumventing the city/
country debate, encapsulating his claim that Murray has always
brought an intricacy of language to his treatment of the bush
which is alien to the tradition, but which 'the Australian bush
has always cried out for'.[12]

At nearly the same time as *The Boys* was receiving this
troubled but admiring reception from its (almost exclusively)
male reviewers, however, the charge of ethnocentricity, which
had risen perhaps most cogently in Catalano's review of *The
Vernacular Republic,* was repeated by Michael Sharkey. Sharkey
felt that Murray had not, despite his proclaimed interest in the
native culture, moved beyond an English Romantic traditionalism, a view of the proper concerns of Australian poetry as being
'derived not so much from an experiential or experimental
consideration of relationships in the Australian landscape and
areas of human behaviour, but from "received" revelation'. This
traditionalism gave Murray, as Sharkey saw it, a 'specious or
patronising' view of the Aborigines (critical flak which Patrick
White was also subject to), as well as a scorn for those city-
dwellers and socialists who did not share his vision of Australia
and his Christianity.[13]

Murray emerged from this time of apparent critical neglect
down to the late 1970s and into the early 1980s, therefore, as a
highly contentious figure on his native ground (and seemingly
deliberately so). His poetic gift, when treating his 'proper'
subjects, was held to set him above other Australian poets, both
contemporary and earlier. Yet, on the other hand, his work was
often preceived to cross the boundaries into political immediacy
and republican advocacy, a feature which was perceived to weaken
it. Further, there were tensions between his proclaimed national
cultural inclusiveness and the manner of the poetry itself.
Through its particularity and difficulty, the very integration it
strove for became complicated, if not actually impossible. The
poetry's own complexity might be a reflection of this awkward
fusion of different interests, but, at the same time, might seem
to exclude those it would seem to wish to engage with its project.
As such, it might seem particularly representative of what Fay

Zwicky was to diagnose in 1985 as 'A Colonial Dilemma'. Although deeply disliking Murray's apparent anti-feminism, Zwicky saw his work, along with Patrick White's, as presenting an understandable prickliness towards its audience (particularly the national one): 'This is a poetry arguing for the virtue of difficult ambitions in a cultural context artistically and intellectually unfavourable to thinking about this world or any other.'[14]

Given the nature of that intractable 'dilemma', the change in tone which greeted Murray's work in the 1980s was partly one which reflected the movement of the poetry away from immediate social and political concerns towards more religious and self-consciously poetic ones. The critical response in Australia, as a result, carried a good deal of relief. There was a critical consensus that the next volume represented a culmination; that, as Dennis Haskell put it, Murray has been 'for many years ... Australia's most important, and controversial, poet'. 'The People's Otherworld could readily be seen as the work towards which Murray's other books have built.'[15] Whilst Page, in the review cited at the start of this chapter, noted the continued 'dismissal of, if not exactly contempt for, many of those who do not see things as he does', he also recognized the 'compassion' in poems such as 'The Steel', one of the elegies for Murray's mother. Carmel Gaffney, on the other hand, was as unreservedly praising as Haskell, focusing on the religious resonance which had become more explicit in the poetry: 'Murray's originality and his ability to present philosophical and theological concepts in concrete images not only revivifies traditional concepts but extends them.'[16]

A year earlier, David Malouf had meditated upon the virtues of a distinctive Australian tradition of poetry in ways that set Murray as 'prime exemplar', through those very qualities implied by the title of The People's Otherworld. These virtues included

> A concern with permanence ... a belief that the best values
> are quiet, common, even commonplace, and that they are
> best spoken for from the centre rather than the extremes
> ... a belief that the poet ought not to claim too much for

his own insights and that he should speak sociably, using common language and the middle voice.

Whilst he acknowledged that the difficulty of Murray's poetry, 'the density of his argument', established a tension between his recent work and that traditional ideal (Murray 'is the most thoroughgoingly intellectual of our poets'), Malouf accorded his writing pride of place in continuing and extending the tradition's characteristic values.[17]

Throughout the rest of the 1980s, this sense of the centrality of Murray's work within national writing, and of his predominance through the original brilliance of the poetry, grew rapidly – perhaps marking the partial recession at the time of claims for a native postmodernism on the American model. The perceived 'contradictions' in his thinking and work were consistently acknowledged, but subsumed under admiration for the achievement itself. During this time also, Murray built a steady, if not initially spectacular, *international* reputation, with each new volume receiving some attention in the main British literary magazines, and with the publication of his collections by the Carcanet Press in Manchester, England. His work also received some attention in the United States, but this was to grow more steadily in the 1990s.

So, in a review of *The Daylight Moon* (1987) in *Overland*, Keith Russell saw the poems on Murray's return to the home place at Bunyah as part of a wider generational urge for those – including Clive James and Germaine Greer – who had attended university at Sydney in the late 1950s and early 1960s, and who were at this time also in various ways looking to come back home. 'If Murray's generation is the first to genuinely belong in Australia,' Russell argued, 'then it does so by locating the spiritual dimension in bits and pieces of *real estate* ... the poetry is a bush hideout.' The shift towards possession of the land was, this critic felt, the true new development in Murray's work, rather than the interest in narrative signalled on the book's cover. As a result of his relocation, the polemical side of Murray's work had become softened.[18] The New Zealand poet and critic C.K. Stead, writing in the *London Review of Books* about *The Daylight Moon* and the recently published Carcanet edition of the *Selected Poems*, made elaborate play on the abounding circumstantial 'contradictions' in Murray: 'The writer who insists on an Australian consciousness and the severing of ties with the Mother Country is obsessed with his Scots ancestry and the Celtic literary inheritance.' But, when writing of the impact of the poetry in *The Daylight Moon* itself, Stead became extremely enthusiastic: 'It is wonderfully disciplined writing, offering what poetry and nothing else can offer, an art that arrests one's otherwise frustrated sense of the richness of life.'[19]

The growth of serious critical attention afforded Murray throughout the 1980s was marked also by an (albeit as yet small) increase in the number of articles on his work published in Australia. Jennifer Strauss added an interesting, if deliberately tendentious, element to the debate about Murray's polemicism by attaching it to a masculine tradition unable, as in his poems in memory of his mother, to see the world from the woman's point of view.[20] Then, in 1989, the poet and critic Kevin Hart produced what remains perhaps the most generous, understanding and intelligent essay on Murray's work, '"Interest" in Les A. Murray'. Hart addressed from a different angle what had become the abiding (if gradually lessening) critical concern with Murray's work – the way the poetry seemed to be consistently devalued by its engagement with politics and polemic.

Perceiving that Murray's 'abiding interest is in integration, in convergences', Hart saw as inevitable the condemnations of those the poet perceived as socially divisive, including Marxists and feminists. Rather, as exemplified by *Poems Against Economics*, Murray accorded a privileged position to the work of art, a special economy which lifts the work above such division and looks down upon it. For Murray, as Hart saw it, art 'is an *enactment* of cultural fusion, a "complete utterance" that mysteriously integrates all aspects of the experience ... In other words, true art is apolitical, and a political response to art ... would misvalue the work.'

Because of this contradictorily prosaic *and* poetic economy operative in Murray, Hart saw him as thinking within an overly narrow and contradictory understanding of ideology as a matter of personal choice, rather than as something imbuing the times. When, from the mid-1970s and *Ethnic Radio* onwards, it seemed that the nascent republic was being pulled in directions unsympathetic to Murray's beliefs (for both national and international reasons), his poetry was condemned to operate increasingly at the level of narrow ideology, to lose its poetic force. And yet, at the end of the essay, Hart brilliantly returned upon his own insights, and defined the true value of Murray's work in and for the Australian context:

> in [his] poetry, at least, Australian literary culture is underdetermined … Context determines meaning, to be sure, but Murray is partly responsible for making that context in the first place. In showing that his proper name functions in a new context, that context becomes a natural part of our cultural identity, one we have simply not noticed before. Reading Murray, one is always following a circulation of texts and contexts, not only texts participating in contexts, but, just as often, texts trying to make their own contexts.[21]

When reviewing Murray's next collection, *Dog Fox Field* of 1990, Hart returned to the theme of there being two types of writing by Murray. Taking the book's central preoccupation as the relation between the conscious mind and the dreaming, imaginative one operative in the brain's 'other hemisphere', Hart identified that dreaming for Murray as 'perhaps in a sense' Australia itself. Yet, reading the more polemical work here, Hart reflected once more that 'Murray works with two poetics: one recreating "our *other* history", and one engaging directly (and often astringently) with ordinary history. In some of Murray's most impressive writing the two poetics are braided together; while his weakest verse tends to work solely in the public register.' For Hart, therefore, *Dog Fox Field* does not contain any great Murray, such as had been realized in 'SMLE' and 'The Buladelah-Taree Holiday Song Cycle'.[22] Conversely, C.K. Stead, in *The London Review of Books*, responded to the sheer Auden-like verbal and formal inventiveness: 'Murray ... has no classic sense of restraint, of tact, of limit. His talent clamours to be fed ... I read him compulsively.' This is a view of Murray's immense talent picked up again by James Wood in his review of *Translations* (1992) in the same journal. Playing what, by now, had become a critical parlour game of aligning Murray with and against an international poetic superleague which also contained the Irishman Seamus Heaney, the West Indian Derek Walcott and the Russian exile Joseph Brodsky, Wood found Murray 'more inventive, much wittier and more agile' than any of these peers.[23]

In Australia itself, Murray's status was confirmed by the appearance of Lawrence Bourke's book-length study *A Vivid Steady State: Les Murray and Australian Poetry*, a work which traces Murray's career through its thematic links with earlier nationalist writers. Preoccupied by the disputes between Murray and the modernist generation in the 1970s, including John Tranter and Robert Adamson, Bourke clearly responded to Murray's 'public affirmative stance, with the refusal to enter into subjective doubt'. However, this is an approach which, although registering Murray's uniqueness within his particular context, rather underplays the creative seeming contradictions and deliberate changes of stance in response to event throughout Murray's oeuvre.[24] Much more valuable, perhaps, is the gathering of essays from both national and international critics and poets in Carmel Gaffney's *Counterbalancing Light*, essays which grapple directly with some of the more contentious aspects of his craft, from his dismissal of the Enlightenment to his politics and religious beliefs.[25]

With the publication of Murray's successive volumes in Britain and the United States, as well as in his own country from the mid-1980s, he attracted a further, and almost wholly admiring, audience. John Greening, for example, greeted *Subhuman Redneck Poems* with the claim that 'Reading this new book is like some venture into the interior, a Vossian epic of effort and observation.'[26] And yet some of the worries in Australian responses to the work were communicated to these new readers.

Robert Crawford, for instance, saw the first Carcanet volume, *The Daylight Moon*, as containing 'a mixture of the finest poems in the English-speaking world in the 1980s', but detected also some moments when 'the pressure of explicit sermonizing ... becomes a threat' to the poetic integrity.[27] However, all of these publications of the 1990s on Murray, both in Australia and abroad, carry the weight of Andrew Taylor's assessment, when reviewing the selected prose published in his country, *A Working Forest*, of Murray as an 'experimental and innovative' writer at the forefront of his country's poetry, and pursuing a path very much his own: 'All good poets must cleave to their own vision.'[28]

In their seminal work *The Empire Writes Back*, the three Australian critics and theorists Bill Ashcroft, Gareth Griffiths and Helen Tiffin acclaim Murray's poetry as a paradigmatic instance of mature postcolonial writing founded on the settler condition, one free of 'the metropolitan discourse imposed during the imperial period':

> A writer like Murray is the archetypal ethnographer whose cultural location 'creates' two audiences and faces two directions, wishing to reconstitute experience through an act of writing which uses the tools of one culture or society [i.e., for him, the British] and yet seeks to remain faithful to the experience of another.[29]

Whilst this might describe a generalized *impetus* in Murray, it fails to establish either the local *specificities* of his enterprise, or the multivalent strands of address his poetry makes. As Derek Walcott, himself a poet of complex inheritance and utterance, has argued, this view of Murray as a poet of binaries within a larger post-colonial literary and theoretical context is itself too constricted: 'The rush and sputter of the line ... are like technical fireworks, and their successive explosions can only be managed exactly by imagining Murray's own voice'.[30]

What I hope has emerged from this study are both the excitement and the sense of risk and affront within Murray's version of an idealized, polydialectical, poetic voice, one that speaks for international *and* republican conditions in the twenty-first century. Various strands within his thinking – from the Boeotian, to the synthetic 'organic' amalgamation of Boeotian and Athenian, to the adoption of written English models of Aborigine orality, to the Gaelic, the republican, and the Catholic/religious – have been put forward at various points, in various combinations, throughout his career. He has remained in conscious and contentious dialogue with debates about national emergence almost from the outset, bringing his own version of complex and distinctive nationalism to bear on what he sees as blindness, partiality, or cultural and class prejudice. To this extent, and given his temporary but deliberate adoption of masks of self-delighting bloody-mindedness, he performs a traditional, bardic, role in his society, and for this reason is in line to be even more widely recognized in years to come.

Yet he has also consistently written with both verve and humour in addressing this issue of national distinctiveness – his love of obliqueness, odd facts, and riddling often brings a tone of wryness to the writing. More particularly, his unabashed celebration of particular aspects of Australian tradition and life, the new perspectives from the New World which have opened, has proved vital in moving his country's literature beyond that 'cultural cringe' towards Europe which had dogged it, and which had even perhaps been exacerbated by the metropolitan perspectives of the generation of writers immediately preceding his, including, perhaps paradoxically, his most famous predecessor, Patrick White. To that extent, Murray has been central in moving political and cultural debate onwards, using his highly personalized and synthetic version of the 'nation' as a point of discussion. This ambitious project, and Murray's concurrently wonderful and wide-ranging linguistic and poetic abilities, eventually achieved its moment when, in the late 1980s, Bruce Bennett could conclude that 'Les Murray's vision of Australia had received widespread recognition.'[31]

Notes

Chapter 1

1 Paul Carter, *Living in a New Country: History, Travelling and Language* (London: Faber, 1992), 2.

2 Judith Wright, *Preoccupations in Australian Poetry* (Melbourne: Oxford University Press, 1965), xi.

3 Ania Loomba, *Colonialism/Postcolonialism* (London: Routledge, 1998), 9–10.

4 Paul Kane, *Australian Poetry: Romanticism and Negativity* (Cambridge: Cambridge University Press, 1996), 35.

5 Geoffrey Bolton, *The Oxford History of Australia, Volume 5: 1942–1988: The Middle Way* (Melbourne: Oxford University Press, 1990), 235.

6 Terry Goldie, 'Signifier Resignified: Aborigines in Australian Literature', in Anna Rutherford (ed.), *Aboriginal Culture Today* (Sydney: Dangeroo, 1988), 70.

7 Kevin Hart, '"Interest" in Les A. Murray', *Australian Literary Studies*, Vol. 14, No. 2, October 1989, 156.

8 *The Jindyworobaks*, selected and ed. Brian Elliott (St Lucia: University of Queensland Press, 1979), xx–xxvii *passim*.

9 In an uncollected review of 1973, 'Getting to Know the Landscape', (*Sydney Morning Herald*, 25 August) Murray had argued for this twofold vision: 'Man does and will change country as much out of creativity as out of physical need. We therefore have to learn to evaluate environments sensitively.'

10 Peter Porter, *Collected Poems* (Oxford: Oxford University Press, 1983), 212.

11 In a review, 'The Paradox of Technology', (*Sydney Morning*

Herald, 31 August 1974, 17) Murray described the paradox 'of man's technology, at once powerful and banal, threatening and yet capable of creating, and revealing, great beauty.' Richard White has seen fascination with technology as an attribute of the Australian 'national type', the ways in which Australians have figured their distinctive identity across history, in a masculine 'identification with new technology, a love of machines, a sort of schoolboy's interest in ships and cars and planes' (*Inventing Australia: Images and Identity 1688–1980* (Sydney: George Allen & Unwin, 1981), 83.

12   'Who's Ignatius, Whose Loyola', *Kunapipi*, Vol. 1, No. 2, 1979, 149.

13   Sue Rowley, 'Australian Bush Mythology' in Kate Darian-Smith, Liz Gunner and Sarah Nuttall (eds), *Text, Theory, Space: Land, Literature and History in South Africa and Australia* (London: Routledge, 1996), 134.

14   Carter, *Living in a New Country*, 24.

15   Bill Ashcroft, Gareth Griffiths and Helen Tiffin have argued that 'in settler cultures, even more than in post-colonial societies, abrogation [of the colonizer's language and cultural traits] will almost certainly not be total within the speaking community' (*The Empire Writes Back: Theory and Practice in Post-Colonial Literatures* (London: Routledge, 1989), 75.

16   *Killing the Black Dog: Essay and Poems* (Annandale, New South Wales: The Federation Press, 1997), 19.

17   Richard White has discussed this element of the 'national type', but also the fear attending it, as 'an emphasis … on masculinity, and on masculine friendships and teamwork, or "mateship" … women were portrayed as a negation of the type, at best one who passively pined and waited, at worst as one who would drag a man down' (*Inventing Australia*, 83).

18   Kay Schaffer, *Women and the Bush: Forces of Desire in Australian Culture* (Cambridge, Cambridge University Press, 1988), 123–4.

19   *The Quality of Sprawl: Thoughts About Australia* (Potts Point, New South Wales: Duffy and Snellgrove, 1999), 235.

20   Ashcroft, et al., *The Empire Writes Back*, 47.

21   Bolton, *Oxford History of Australia*, 174.

22   *The Quality of Sprawl*, 217, 225, 224.

23   J.S. Manifold, *Who Wrote the Ballads? Notes on Australian Folksong* (Sydney: Australasian Book Society, 1964), 24.

24   G.A. Wilkes, *The Stockyard and the Croquet Lawn: Literary*

Evidence for Australian Cultural Development (London: Edward Arnold, 1981), 36, 38, 44.

25 Benedict Anderson, *Imagined Communities: Reflections on the Origin and Spread of Nationalism* (London: Verso, 1983; rev. ed. 1991), 5–7.

26 'Of Working People', *Sydney Morning Herald*, 10 August 1974, 15. In this emphasis on the many-mindedness of Australian writing, Murray is reflecting distinguishing ideas long expressed in the country. In 1890, Professor E.E. Morris had condemned the 'weird melancholy' tone of writing favoured at the time by followers of the novelist Marcus Clarke as too European, and was glad that 'the great body of our nascent literature is cheerful and vigorous, as becomes the pioneer writers of a young and hopeful country' (John Barnes (ed.), *The Writer in Australia: A Collection of Literary Documents 1856 to 1964* (Melbourne: Oxford University Press, 1969), 44–5.

27 Lawrence Bourke, 'Les A. Murray', *Journal of Commonwealth Literature*, Vol. 21, No. 1, 1986, 179.

28 John Barnes (ed.), *The Penguin Henry Lawson Short Stories* (Ringwood, Victoria, 1986), 34.

29 Helen Frizell, 'Les Murray Takes Off', *Sydney Morning Herald*, 23 February 1980, 17.

30 When reviewing a tribute book for Auden, Murray saw the latter's death as bringing to an end the centred world of English and American literature: 'The power structure of literature is fragmented – not enough yet, but it's coming ...'. His ambition was, of necessity, to be a prominent figure in that alternative centring, following on from the older poet's death ('A World that has Passed Away', *Sydney Morning Herald* (2 August 1975), p. 17).

31 Richard White has said persuasively that 'There is no "real" Australia waiting to be uncovered. A national identity is an invention ... When we look at ideas about national identity, we need to ask, not whether they are true or false, but what their function is, whose creation they are, and whose interests they serve' (*Inventing Australia*, viii).

32 *Fivefathers: Five Australian Poets of the Pre-academic Era* (Manchester: Carcanet, 1994), 17, 20.

33 In interview, though, Murray has shown that even this view is contingent upon his wider considerations: 'I have been called anti-modernist. That is going too far. I am having a *conversation* with modernism. I have been afraid of being imprisoned in a particular

style, so I have moved further beyond the influence of Eliot than
my contemporaries. I didn't want my poetry to be an adjunct to
my despair: I wanted it to return to a fuller emotional range.' (Max
Davidson, 'Poet Laureate of the Australian Bush', *The Daily
Telegraph*, 18 April 1997, 27).

34   *Fivefathers*, 52.

35   Andrew Taylor, *Reading Australian Poetry* (Queensland:
University of Queensland Press, 1987), 68.

36   *Fivefathers*, 23.

37   Paul Carter, *The Road to Botany Bay: An Essay in Spatial History*
(London: Faber, 1987), 36, 40.

38   Thomas W. Shapcott (ed.), *Australian Poetry Now* (Melbourne:
Sun Books, 1970), ix.

39   Ibid., 74.

40   Joan Kirkby (ed.), *The American Model: Influence and Independence in Australian Poetry* (Sydney: Hall and Iremonger), 1972.

41   In her book *A Question of Commitment: Australian Literature in
the Twenty Years After the War* (Sydney: Allen & Unwin, 1989,
9–20), Susan McKernan has argued that it was the threat of
invasion which led to a resurgence of nationalist tradition
throughout the 1940s, with a particular valuing of Lawson as a
left-wing democratic socialist. This tradition was then compounded
during the Cold War. Murray's thinking clearly was sparked by,
and continues on other ground, a similar reaction within and to the
tradition.

42   Bolton, *Oxford History of Australia*, 167–77 *passim*.

43   'Les Murray: An Interview with Carole Oles', *American Poetry
Review*, Vol. 15, No. 2, March/April 1986, 31.

44   Homi K. Bhabha, *The Location of Culture* (London: Routledge,
1994), 63.

45   John Tranter, 'A Warrier Poet, Still Living at Anzac Cove', *The
Australian* (29 January 1977), 27.

46   David A. Kent, 'From Sudan to Saigon: A Critical Review of
Historical Works', *Australian Literary Studies*, Vol. 12 No. 2,
October 1995, 155, 268.

Chapter 2

1   In reviewing *The Ilex Tree* in *The London Magazine* (January 1967, 87), Roy Fuller noted the 'entirely unself-conscious' sophistication of the work of both poets. Although he preferred Lehmann's contribution, finding Murray's work a bit too restrained, Fuller noted that Murray 'leans on no other poet', and that both writers 'convey no sense of provincialism; indeed they confidently use the perspectives of past generations, place-names, and so forth'.

2   Bolton, *Oxford History of Australia*, 183.

3   'Our Best Customer', *Sydney Morning Herald* (23 June 197, 21). In defence of Murray's view, one may cite historians such as Annette Hamilton, who sees the fate of Australian POWs on the Burma-Thailand Railway in 1942–45 as 'one of the cruellest episodes for Australia in a military history full of awful events' ('Skeletons of Empire: Australians and the Burma-Thailand Railway', in Kate Darian-Smith and Paula Hamilton [eds], *Memory and History in Twentieth-Century Australia* (Melbourne: Oxford University Press, 1994, 93).

4   This was the first line of the sequence in the original version, which was moved to the opening of section 2 in the revisions for the *Collected Poems*.

5   An important change in the first section of this version also alters the original 'clumsy son' who refuses to dance with his father into someone who only dances *'on bits of paper'*. The poet's role is now fully accepted, but a further marker of distance from this first place is also established.

6   Manning Clark, *History of Australia*, abridged by Michael Cathcart (London: Chatto & Windus, 1994), 68.

Chapter 3

1   'The Flag Rave', *PM*, 237. Murray recalls that one of 'the most attractive' of the variants of flags that he considered contained 'a line rayonny of seven points'. He adds that, at this stage, he found doodling possible flags 'an aid to meditation while writing poems' (239).

2   For a useful discussion of Murray's consistent attitudes in this area, see Bert Almon, 'Les Murray's Critique of the Enlightenment',

in Carmel Gaffney (ed.), *Counterbalancing Light: Essays on the Poetry of Les Murray* (Armidale: Kardoorair Press, 1997), 1–19.

3   In the earliest published article on Murray, Dianne Ailwood had noted similar traits in his work around 1970, a movement away from the 'comparative formality' of the first two collections towards a sense of 'Australian regeneration' which involved a 'conventional' but 'complex' and 'awkward' syntax reminiscent of 'unrehearsed speech' ('The Poetry of Les Murray', *Southerly*, No. 3, 1971, 190). Richard White (*Inventing Australia*, 153) has noted that qualities of proclaimed national uniqueness similar to those given by Murray in 'The Completed Australian' have emerged throughout Australian history from the nineteenth century, particularly at a time of national crisis. He quotes from an article from the 'Crisis Issue' of the magazine *Meanjin* in 1942, at the time when Australia might have been invaded by Japan, as arguing for 'an Australia of the spirit ... Sardonic, idealist, tongue-tied perhaps, it is the Australia of all who truly belong here.'

4   Bhabha, *The Location of Culture*, 83, 142, 186, 243.

5   Clark, *History of Australia*, 49.

6   In the essay 'The Human-Hair Thread' (1977), which Murray was later to omit from a selection of his prose writings in Australia, *A Working Forest*, 'because it is over-explanatory about [his] own work', he had in a more general comment praised Berndt for his rendering of 'Aboriginal poetry into a language deeply in tune with the best Australian vernacular speech, and [which] reveals affinities' (*PT*, 92).

7   Many, of course, in the country have seen Murray's version of cultural multiplicity, despite such caveats, as limited – Gregory Mellenish, for instance, already in 'Les Murray's Vernacular Republic: A Reply', wrote that the poet's ideal was 'an arrogant, monolingual nation with a culture built from ... poverty' (*Quadrant*, 20, August 1976, 36). But there is a paradox here, in that all nationalisms, if we are to follow Benedict Anderson, are derived from European models of post-feudal rule with local additions. They are inevitably therefore, whatever the racial origins of those promulgating them, partial and selective (*Imagined Communities*, 6–7).

Chapter 4

1 Murray might be remembering here an incident in the protests against the Vietnam War, when, on 6 June 1966, a woman threw or smeared 'blood' (in fact red paint) over a parade of returning veterans. The incident entered Australian folk memory, although the allegiances of the woman herself, Nadine Jensen, have never become clear – she was a part of neither the feminist nor the anti-war movements. See Ann Curthoys, '"Vietnam": Public Memory of an Anti-War Movement', in Darian-Smith and Hamilton (eds), *Memory and History in Twentieth-Century Australia*, 128–9.

2 Clark, *History of Australia*, 461.

3 *The Australian Year: The Chronicle of Our Seasons and Celebrations*, with photographs by Peter Solness and others (New South Wales: Angus & Robertson, 1985), 12.

4 In his *Identifying Poets: Self and Territory in Twentieth-Century Poets* (Edinburgh: Edinburgh University Press, 1993), 91–2, Robert Crawford has some pertinent remarks on Murray's use of the motif of travel as a form of continuing presence.

5 Murray's advocacy of a neglected early nineteenth century work by Frank 'the Poet' Macnamara focuses upon similar issues of diction: 'The poem draws on many registers, from legalese … and contemporary literary diction … to sporting vernacular and slang … but its ruling voice is a middle one, made to be shared widely. This very use of language also enacts the humane vision of the poem' ('A Folk Inferno', 1988, *PT*, 321).

6 To that extent, Rolls's prose shares some of the qualities of the 'poetic' history which 'The Human-Hair Thread' attributes to the Aborigines – 'a matter of significant moments rather than of development. To make it historical in our sense requires an imposition of Western thinking' (*PT*, 95).

Chapter 5

1 Robert Crawford, 'Les Murray's "Present Sequence"', in Gaffney (ed.), *Counterbalancing Light*, 66.

2 Jamie Grant, 'Subhuman Redneck Politics', *Southerly*, Vol. 58, No. 2, Winter 1998, 126, 130.

3 Edna Longley, 'Introductory Reflections', in Warwick Gould and Edna Longley (eds), *That Accusing Eye: Yeats and His Irish*

Readers, Yeats Annual, No. 12 (Basingstoke: Macmillan, 1996), 13.

4 Martin Leer saw the book as offering 'not political satire ... but the voicing of a deep despair and loneliness, not just of an individual but of an entire class or culture' ('Erocide and Milder Love', *Planet*, 124, August–September 1997, 104–6).

5 Murray has described his own being bullied at Taree High School, for being 'a dreamy fat hill-billy kid', in a piece published in 1988, 'From Bulby Bush to Figure City' (*PT*, 339).

6 In a review for the British paper the *Independent*, Peter Porter says that the violence is 'purveyed in an awesomely mimetic poetry. ... There can never have been a verse novel quite like this. It seems to me as impressive as it often is repulsive' (Saturday Magazine, 4 July 1998, 9).

7 Salman Rushdie, *Imaginary Homelands* (London: Granta, 1991); Bhabha, *The Location of Culture*, 224. For a full discussion of migrancy in postcolonial texts, see Elleke Boehmer, *Colonial and Postcolonial Literature* (Oxford: Oxford University Press, 1995), 232–43.

Chapter 6

1 Geoff Page, 'Les Murray's "Otherworld"', *Quadrant*, Vol. 28, Nos. 1–2, January–February 1984, 124.

2 Christopher Pollnitz, 'The Bardic Pose: A Survey of Les A. Murray's Poetry I', *Southerly*, Vol. 40, No. 4, December 1980, 367.

3 Robert Gray, 'Garlands of Ilex', *Poetry Australia*, Vol. 70, May 1979, 67.

4 David Malouf, 'Subjects Found and Taken Up', *Poetry Australia*, Vol. 57, December 1975, 70–1.

5 Ronald Dunlop, 'Recent Australian Poetry', *Poetry Australia*, Vol. 32, February 1970, 51.

6 Roger McDonald, 'Bending the Road a Little With Personal History', *Poetry Australia*, Vol. 47, 1973, 71.

7 Penelope Nelson, 'Listening to Lives: Les A. Murray's Vernacular Republic', *Poetry Australia*, Vol. 64, October 1977, 74, 77.

8 Gary Catalano, '"Evading the Modernities": The Poetry of Les A. Murray', *Meanjin*, Vol. 36, No. 1, May 1977, 70.

9   Gary Catalano, 'Stroking it Open: A Poetry Chronicle', *Meanjin*, Vol. 39, No. 3, October 1980, 351–3.

10 Christopher Pollnitz, 'The Bardic Pose: A Survey of Les A. Murray's Poetry III', *Southerly*, Vol. 41, No. 2, June 1981, 208–9.

11 C.J. Koch, 'Les Murray's Watershed', *Quadrant*, Vol. 24, No. 9, 1980, 40–1.

12 Peter Porter, 'Les Murray: An Appreciation', *Journal of Commonwealth Literature*, Vol. 17, No. 1, 1982, 45–6.

13 Michael Sharkey, 'Les Murray's Single-Minded Many Sidedness', *Overland*, Vol. 82, 1980, 19–21. The sense of Murray's place in tradition, this time uncharged with politic argumentation, would re-emerge in Paul Kane's reading of him in *Australian Poetry: Romanticism and Negativity* (Cambridge: Cambridge University Press, 1996).

14 Fay Zwicky, 'Language or Speech? A Colonial Dilemma', *Overland*, Vol. 98, April 1985, 45.

15 Dennis Haskell, 'Bringing the C20 to Bay: The People's Otherworld', *Westerly*, Vol. 29, No. 4, December 1984, 75.

16 Carmel Gaffney, 'Les Murray's Otherworld', *Quadrant*, Vol. 28, Nos. 7–8, July–August 1984, 55.

17 David Malouf, 'Some Volumes of Selected Poems of the 1970s, II', *Australian Literary Studies*, Vol. 10, No. 3, May 1982, 301, 308.

18 Keith Russell, 'The Drum of Return', *Overland*, Vol. 110, March 1988, 82.

19 C.K. Stead, 'Les Murray: Authentic Oz', *Answering to the Language: Essays on Modern Writers* (Auckland: Auckland University Press, 1989), 125, 132.

20 Jennifer Strauss, 'Elegies for Mothers: Reflections on Gwen Harwood's "Mother Who Gave Me Life" and Les Murray's "Three Poems in Memory of My Mother"', *Westerly*, Vol. 34, No. 4, December 1989, 58–63.

21 Kevin Hart, '"Interest" in Les A. Murray', *Australian Literary Studies*, Vol. 14, No. 2, October 1989, 148, 159.

22 Kevin Hart, 'Dog Fox Field', *Overland*, Vol. 122, 1991, 71.

23 C.K. Stead, 'Ancient Orthodoxies', *London Review of Books*, 23 May 1991, 10; James Wood, 'Jihad', 15 August 1993, 14.

24 Lawrence Bourke, *A Vivid Steady State: Les Murray and Australian Poetry* (New South Wales: New South Wales University Press, 1992), 53.

25 Gaffney, *Counterbalancing Light*, 1997.

26 John Greening, 'Les Murray: *Subhuman Redneck Poems*', *Poetry Wales*, Vol. 33, No. 1, July 1997, 62–3.

27 Robert Crawford, 'An Australian Ithaca', *Krino*, No. 5, Spring 1988, 16–17.

28 Andrew Taylor, 'Noonday Axeman', *Australian Book Review*, Vol. 193, August 1997, 5.

29 Ashcroft et al., *The Empire Writes Back*, 60–1. See also Boehmer, *Colonial and Postcolonial Literature*, 206–13.

30 Derek Walcott, 'Crocodile Dandy: Les Murray', in *What the Twilight Says* (London: Faber, 1998), 189.

31 Bruce Bennett, 'Perceptions of Australia 1965–1988', Laurie Hergenhan (ed.), *The Penguin New Literary History of Australia* (Ringwood: Penguin, 1988), 444.

Bibliography

Works by Les Murray

POETRY

The Ilex Tree, with Geoffrey Lehmann, Canberra: National University Press, 1965.

The Weatherboard Cathedral, Sydney: Angus and Robertson, 1969.

Poems Against Economics, Sydney: Angus and Robertson, 1972.

Lunch and Counter Lunch, Sydney: Angus and Robertson, 1974.

The Vernacular Republic, Sydney: Angus and Robertson, 1976; revised and enlarged edition, 1988; Edinburgh: Canongate, 1982; New York: Persea, 1983.

Ethnic Radio, Sydney: Angus and Robertson, 1977.

The Boys Who Stole the Funeral, Sydney: Angus and Robertson, 1980; New York: Farrar Straus & Giroux, 1991.

The People's Otherworld, Sydney: Angus and Robertson, 1983.

The Daylight Moon, Sydney: Angus and Robertson, 1987; Manchester: Carcanet, 1987; New York: Persea, 1989.

Dog Fox Field, Sydney: Angus and Robertson, 1990; Manchester: Carcanet, 1990; New York: Farrar Straus & Giroux, 1992.

Collected Poems, Manchester: Carcanet 1991; expanded and corrected edition, 1998.

The Rabbiter's Bounty: Collected Poems, New York: Farrar Straus & Giroux, 1991.

Translations From the Natural World, Melbourne: Heinemann, Australia, 1992; Manchester: Carcanet, 1992; New York: Farrar Straus & Giroux, 1992.

Subhuman Redneck Poems, New South Wales: Duffy and Snellgrove, 1996; Manchester: Carcanet, 1996; New York: Farrar Straus & Giroux, 1997.

Fredy Neptune, New South Wales: Duffy and Snellgrove, 1998; Manchester: Carcanet, 1998; New York: Farrar Straus & Giroux, 1999.

Conscious and Verbal, New South Wales: Duffy and Snellgrove, 1999; Manchester: Carcanet, 1999.

Learning Human: Selected Poems, New York: Farrar Straus & Giroux, 2000.

PROSE COLLECTIONS

The Peasant Mandarin, St Lucia: University of Queensland Press, 1978.

Persistence in Folly, Sydney: Angus and Robertson, 1984.

The Australian Year: The Chronicle of our Seasons and Celebrations, with photographs by Peter Solness and others, New South Wales: Angus and Robertson, 1985.

Blocks and Tackles, Sydney: Angus and Robertson, 1990.

The Paperbark Tree: Selected Prose, Manchester: Carcanet, 1992.

A Working Forest: Selected Prose, Potts Point, New South Wales: Duffy and Snellgrove, 1997.

Killing the Black Dog: Essay and Poems, Annandale, New South Wales: The Federation Press, 1997.

The Quality of Sprawl: Thoughts about Australia, Potts Point, New South Wales: Duffy and Snellgrove, 1999.

EDITED ANTHOLOGIES

The New Oxford Book of Australian Verse, Melbourne: Oxford University Press, 1986.

Anthology of Australian Religious Poetry, Blackburn, Victoria: Collins Dove, 1986.

Fivefathers: Five Australian Poets of the Pre-Academic Era, Manchester: Carcanet, 1994.

UNCOLLECTED PROSE

Statement, *Australian Poetry Now*, Thomas W. Shapcott (ed.), Melbourne: Sun Books, 1970.

Afterword, *12 Poets 1950-1970*, Alexander Craig (ed.), Brisbane: Jacaranda Press, 1971.

Ideas Party, *Bulletin*, 2 December 1972.

Getting to Know the Landscape, *Sydney Morning Herald*, 23 June 1973.

Our Best Customer, *Sydney Morning Herald*, 25 August 1973.

Of Working People, *Sydney Morning Herald*, 10 August 1974.

The Paradox of Technology, *Sydney Morning Herald*, 31 August 1974.

A World That Has Passed Away, *Sydney Morning Herald*, 2 August 1975.

Landscape-as-Identity, *Sydney Morning Herald*, 1 November 1975.

Solitary Soldier, *Sydney Morning Herald*, 8 November 1975.

Poet's Guide, *Sydney Morning Herald*, 7 February 1976.

My New Country Enjoys Good Relations With Death, *Sydney Morning Herald*, 14 February 1976.

The Great Federal Poetry Takeover Plot, *National Times*, 12–17 April 1976.

It Started About 6,000 Years Ago, *Sydney Morning Herald*, 4 September 1976.

Doomster's Day – Or How to Avoid the Apocalypse, *Sydney Morning Herald*, 14 May 1977.

Les Murray, *Quadrant*, August 1977.

Who's Ignatius, Whose Loyola?, *Kunapipi*, Vol. 1, No. 2, 1979.

Posterity Now. Present and Future Texts for Australian Literature, *Island Magazine*, Vol. 8, 1981.

Porter: An Infinitely More Serious Bertie Wooster, *Sydney Morning Herald*, 8 June 1983.

Eulogy for Douglas Stewart, *Southerly*, Vol. 45, No. 2, 1985.

Aphrodite Street, *London Review of Books*, Vol. 10, No. 1, 7 January 1988.

Only a Flat Earth Has Margins: Footnotes on a Deadly Metaphor, *Krino*, No. 18, 1995.

MANUSCRIPTS

Canberra, National Library of Australia, MS 5332.

INTERVIEWS AND PROFILES

Aspects of Life and Language: An Interview, *Krino*, No. 5, Spring 1988.

Baker, Candida. *Yacker 2*, Sydney: Pan, 1987.

Bamforth, Iain. Visiting the Murrays, *PN Review*, Vol. 123, November 1990.

Beaver, Bruce. Murray, Les(lie) A(llan), *Contemporary Poets*, James Vinson (ed.), London and Chicago: St James Press, 1975.

Beeby, Rosslyn. Gold is a Giggle for Poet Les, *Age*, 28 August 1984.

Billen, Andrew. Les miserable, *Observer* (London), 22 June 1997.

Blair, Ron. Les Murray Talks, *24 Hours*, Vol. 1, No. 10, November 1976.

Bourke, Lawrence. Les A. Murray: Interviewed by Lawrence Bourke, *Journal of Commonwealth Literature*, Vol. 21, No. 1, 1986.

Chenery, Susan. The Bard of Bunyah, *Australian*, 4 May 1991.

Crawford, Robert. Les A. Murray Talking with Robert Crawford, *Verse*, No. 5, 1986.

Daly, Martin. Les Murray: A Lot More Than Just Any Old Poet, *The Courier-Mail*, 9 November 1985.

Davidson, Jim. *Sideways from the Page*, Melbourne: Fontana, 1983.

Davidson, Max. Poet Laureate of the Australian Bush, *Daily Telegraph* (London), 18 April 1997.

Ellis, Bob. Those Decadent University Days, *Sydney Morning Herald*, 19 September 1987.

Ferrall, Charles. Bringing the Body into Poetry: An Interview with Les Murray, *New Zealand Books*, Vol. 8, No. 4, October 1998.

Frizell, Helen. Les Murray Takes Off, *Sydney Morning Herald*, 23 February 1980.

Gould, Alan and Page, Geoff. A Wild and Holy Calling: A Conversation with Les A. Murray on Religion and Poetry, *Eremos Newsletter*, Vol. 19, 1987.

Gray, Robert. An Interview with Les Murray, *Quadrant*, Vol. 113, December 1976.

Hauge, Ingvar. Les Murray – en presentasjon, *Vinduet*, Vol. 45, No. 3, 1991.

Headon, David. An Interview with Les Murray, *LiNQ*, Vol. 13, No. 3, 1985.

Hope, Deborah. Murray Goes Back to the Bush to Retrieve Australian Poetry, *Bulletin*, 11 March 1986.

Janakeram, A. Les Murray on Poetry: An Interview, *Rajasthan University Studies in English*, Vol. 20, 1988.

Kavanagh, Paul and Kuch, Peter. An Interview with Les Murray, *Southerly*, Vol. 44, No. 4, 1984.

Kinross Smith, Graeme. The Frequent Image of Farms – A Profile of Les Murray, *Westerly*, No. 3, September 1980.

Matthews, Steven. A Conversation With Les Murray, *PN Review*, Vol. 25, No. 2, November–December 1998.

May, Julian. Poet's Round Table: A Common Language, *PN Review*, Vol. 15, No. 4, 1989.

McGrath, Sandra. An Otherworld of Dreaming in Poetry, *Weekend Australian Magazine*, 5–6 November 1983.

Messing, Daniel. Poetry is Presence. An Interview with Les Murray, *Commonweal*, Vol. 119, No. 10, 22 May, 1992.

Oles, Carole. Les Murray: An Interview, *American Poetry Review*, Vol. 15, No. 2, March/April 1986.

Peacock, Noel. Embracing the Vernacular: An Interview with Les Murray, *Australian and New Zealand Studies in Canada*, Vol. 7, June 1992.

Porter, Peter. Les Murray Interviewed by Peter Porter, *Australian Studies*, Vol. 4, 1990.

Pratt, Noel. Showbiz of the Solitary Man, *Australian*, 7 November 1970.

Rodriguez, Judith. Murray, Les(lie) A(llan), in James Vinson and K.L. Kirkpatrick (eds), *Contemporary Poets*, London and Chicago: St James Press, 1985.

Scammell, William. Interview with Les Murray, *PN Review*, Vol. 110, July–August 1996.

Sharp, Iain. Interview with Les Murray, *Landfall: New Zealand Arts and Letters*, Vol. 42, No. 2, June 1988.

Throsby, Margaret. The Search for 'Ah!', *Look and Listen*, August 1984.

Williams, Barbara. An Interview with Les Murray, *Westerly*, Vol. 37, No. 2, Winter 1992.

—— and Taylor, Andrew. *In Other Words: Interviews with Australian Poets*, Amsterdam: Rodopi, 1998.

Wilmer, Clive. Les Murray in Conversation, *PN Review*, March/April 1992.

Criticism

BOOKS ON MURRAY

Bourke, Lawrence. *A Vivid Steady State: Les Murray and Australian Poetry*, New South Wales: New South Wales University Press, 1992.

Gaffney, Carmel (ed.). *Counterbalancing Light: Essays on the Poetry of Les Murray*, Armidale, New South Wales: Kardoorair Press, 1997.

Nelson, Penelope. *Notes on the Poetry of Les A. Murray*, Sydney: Methuen, 1978.

ESSAYS, CHAPTERS, ARTICLES AND SELECTED MAJOR REVIEWS ON MURRAY

Ailwood, Dianne. 'The Poetry of Les A. Murray', *Southerly*, Vol. 31, 1971.

Alman, Bert. 'Fullness of Being in Les Murray's "Presence: Translations from the Natural World"', *Antipodes*, Vol. 8, No. 2, December 1994.

Bamforth, Iain. 'Physiognomy of a Maximalist – the Poetry of Les Murray', *Verse*, Vol. 6, No. 2, 1989.

Barnie, John. 'The Poetry of Les Murray', *Australian Literary Studies*, Vol. 12, No. 1, May 1985.

Birkerts, Sven. 'The Rococo of his Own Still Centre', *Parnassus*, Vol. 15, No. 2, Summer 1989.

Bourke, Lawrence. '"Digging Under the Horse": Surface As Disguise in the Poetry of Les Murray', *Southerly*, Vol. 32, No. 1, March 1987.

—— 'The Rapture of Place: From Immanence to Transcendence in the Poetry of Les Murray', *Westerly*, Vol. 33, No. 1, March 1988.

Burns, Nicholas. '"Religions are Poems": Spirituality in Les Murray's Poetry', in James S. Scott (ed.), *'And the Birds Began to Sing': Religion and Literature in Post-Colonial Cultures*, Amsterdam: Rodopi, 1996.

Catalano, Gary. 'Evading the Modernities: The Poetry of Les A. Murray', *Meanjin*, Vol. 36, No. 1, 1977.

—— 'Stroking it Open: A Poetry Chronicle', *Meanjin*, Vol. 39, October 1980.

Crawford, Robert. 'An Australian Ithaca', *Krino*, No. 5, Spring 1988.

—— *Identifying Poets: Self and Territory in Twentieth-Century Poetry*, Edinburgh: Edinburgh University Press, 1993.

Dunlop, Ronald. 'Recent Australian Poetry', *Poetry Australia*, Vol. 39, No. 3, February 1970.

Filkins, Peter. 'The Dark and Light of the Daylight Moon: The Poetry of Les Murray', *New England Review*, Vol. 15, No. 3, Summer 1993.

Gaffney, Carmel. 'Les Murray's Otherworld', *Quadrant*, Vol. 28, Nos. 7–8, July–August 1984.

—— 'Les Murray Again: *The Boys Who Stole the Funeral*, A Many Splendid Thing', *Quadrant*, Vol. 32, Nos. 1–2, January–February 1988.

—— '"This Country is My Mind"', *Westerly*, Vol. 39, No. 1, Autumn 1994.

Goodwin, K.L. 'Les Murray, "Toward the Imminent Days"', in P.K. Elkin (ed.), *Australian Poems in Perspective*, St Lucia: University of Queensland Press, 1978.

Gould, Alan. 'With the Distinct Timbre of an Australian Voice', *Antipodes*, Vol. 16, No. 2, December 1992.

Grant, Jamie. 'Subhuman Redneck Politics', *Southerly*, Vol. 58, No. 2, Winter 1998.

Gray, Robert. 'On Every Page is Distilled Some Pleasure in Life', *Sydney Morning Herald*, 11 September 1976.

—— 'Garlands of Ilex', *Poetry Australia*, Vol. 70, May 1979.

Greening, John. 'Les Murray: *Subhuman Redneck Poems*', *Poetry Wales*, Vol. 33, No. 1, July 1997.

Hall, Marlene. 'Les Murray's *Vernacular Republic*', in Jan Fox and Brian MacFarlane (eds), *Perspectives 79: HSC English*, Melbourne: Sorrett Publishing, 1978.

Harrison, Martin. 'Land and Theory', *Southerly*, Vol. 57, No. 2, Winter 1997.

Hart, Kevin. '"Interest" in Les A. Murray', *Australian Literary Studies*, Vol. 14, No. 2, October 1989.

Haskell, Dennis. 'Bringing the C20 to Bay', *Westerly*, No. 4, 1984.

Headon, David. 'Naming the Landscape: Les Murray's Literary Language', *Westerly*, Vol. 28, No. 1, March 1983.

Hergenhan, Laurie. 'War in Post-1960s Fiction: Johnston, Stow, McDonald, Malouf and Les Murray', *Australian Literary Studies*, Vol. 12, No. 2, October 1985.

James, Clive. 'His Brilliant Career', *New York Review of Books*, Vol. 30, No. 6, 14 April 1983.

Kane, Paul. 'Relegation and Convergence', in Robert L. Ross (ed.), *International Literature in English: Essays on the Major Writers*, New York: Garland, 1991.

—— *Australian Poetry: Romanticism and Negativity*, Cambridge: Cambridge University Press, 1996.

Kock, C.J. 'Les Murray's Watershed', *Quadrant*, Vol. 157, 1980.

Leer, Martin. '"Contour-Line by Contour"': Landscape Change as an Index of History in the Poetry of Les Murray', *Australian Literary Studies*, Vol. 16, No. 3, May 1994.

—— 'Erocide and Milder Love', *Planet*, Vol. 124, August/September 1997.

MacLeod, Mark. 'Soundings in Middle Australia', *Meanjin*, Vol. 39, No. 1, April 1980.

Malouf, David. 'Subjects Found and Taken Up', *Poetry Australia*, Vol. 57, December 1975.

—— 'Some Volumes of Selected Poems of the 1970s', II, *Australian Literary Studies*, Vol. 10, No. 3, May 1982.

Marsden, Peter H. 'Paradise Mislaid: The Hostile Reception of Les Murray's Poem "The Liberated Plague"', in Geoffrey V. Davis and Hena Maes-Jelinek (eds), *Crisis and Creativity in the New Literatures in English: Cross/Cultures*, Amsterdam: Rodopi, 1990.

McDonald, Roger. 'Bending the Road a Little With Personal History', *Poetry Australia*, Vol. 47, 1973.

Mellenish, Gregory. 'Les Murray's Vernacular Republic: A Reply', *Quadrant*, Vol. 20, August 1976.

Nelson, Penelope. 'Listening to Lives: Les A. Murray's Vernacular Republic', *Poetry Australia*, Vol. 64, 1977.

O'Connor, Mark. 'Boeotian and Loyolan Art', *Kunapipi*, Vol. 1, No. 1, 1979.

Page, Geoff. 'Les Murray's "Otherworld"', *Quadrant*, Vol. 28, Nos. 1–2, January–February 1984.

Pollnitz, Christopher. 'The Bardic Pose: A Survey of Les A. Murray's Poetry', 1–3 parts in *Southerly*, Vol. 40, No. 4, December 1980; Vol. 41, No. 1, March 1981; Vol. 41, No. 2, June 1981.

Porter, Peter, 'Country Poetry and Town Poetry: A Debate with Les Murray', *Australian Literary Studies*, Vol. 9, May 1979.

—— 'The Muse in the Outback', *Observer Review*, 17 May 1981.

—— 'Les Murray: An Appreciation', *Journal of Commonwealth Literature*, Vol. 17, No. 1, 1982.

—— 'The Map of the Murray', *Scripsi*, Vol. 4, No. 2, November 1986.

—— 'The Wizard of Oz', *Independent Saturday Magazine*, 4 July 1998.

Quartermaine, Peter (ed.). *Diversity Itself: Essays in Australian Arts and Culture*, Exeter: University of Exeter Press, 1986.

Redmond, John. 'Backing into the Outback', *Metre*, No. 2, 1997.

Roberts, Neil. *Narrative and Voice in Postwar Poetry*, London: Longman, 1999.

Ross, Bruce Clunies. 'Les Murray's *The Boys Who Stole the Funeral*', *Recherches Anglaises et Nord-Americannes*, Vol. 21, 1988.

—— 'Fiction and Poetry: Les Murray's *The Boys Who Stole the Funeral*', in Eric Jacobsen, Jorgen Enk Nieson, B.C. Ross, James Stewart (eds), *Studies in Modern Fiction*, Copenhagen: University of Copenhagen, 1990.

—— 'A Poetic Novel for the Vernacular Republic', in Alan Brissenden (ed.) *Aspects of Australian Fiction*, Nedlands: University of Western Australia Press, 1990.

Rowe, Noel. 'Les Murray and the Unseen Opponent', *Southerly*, Vol. 51, No. 2, June 1991.

Rowlands, Graham. 'Behind the Weatherboard Mask', *Nation Review*, 6–12 October 1978.

Shapcott, Thomas. 'John Tranter and Les Murray', *Australian Literary Studies*, Vol. 10, May 1982.

Sharkey, Michael. 'Les Murray's Single-Minded Many-Sidedness', *Overland*, Vol. 82, December 1980.

Sharma, Anurag. 'The Image of India in Les Murray's Poetry', *The Literary Criterion*, Vol. 25, No. 2, 1990.

—— 'The Cow in Les Murray's Poetry', *Rajasthan University Studies in English*, Vol. 23, 1991–92.

—— 'Les Murray's Indianness: The Celebratory Mode of his Poetry, An Analysis of Some of His Indian Poems', *Literary Criterion*, Vol. 27, Nos. 1–2, 1992.

Singh, Kirpal. 'Landscape as Revelation: The Poetry of Les Murray', in A.L. McLeod (ed.), *Subjects Worthy of Fame*, New Delhi: Sterling, 1989.

Stead, C.K. 'Les Murray: Authentic Oz', *Answering to the Language:*

Essays on Modern Writers, Auckland: Auckland University Press, 1989.

Stewart, James. 'In the Land of Cows-to-Milk: On Sitting Back and Thinking of Murray's Boeotia', *Angles on the English Speaking World*, Vol. 2, 1987.

Strauss, Jennifer. 'Elegies for Mothers: Reflections on Gwen Harwood's "Mother Who Gave Me Life" and Les Murray's "Three Poems in Memory of My Mother"', *Westerly*, Vol. 34, No. 4, December 1989.

Talbot, Norman. 'The Buladelah-Taree Holiday Song Cycle', in Norman Talbot (ed.), *Companion to this Place*, Newcastle: Nimrod, 1980.

Taylor, Andrew. 'Time and the Long Poem in Australia', *Westerly*, Vol. 24, No. 4, December 1979.

—— 'Past Imperfect? The Sense of the Past in Les A. Murray', *Reading Australian Poetry*, St Lucia: University of Queensland Press, 1987.

—— 'Noonday Axeman', *Australian Book Review*, No. 193, August 1997.

Tranter, John. 'Anchored in the Local Earth', *Australian*, 2 November 1974.

—— 'Warrior Poet Living Still at Anzac Cove', *Australian*, 29 January 1977.

Walcott, Derek. 'Crocodile Dandy: Les Murray', *What the Twilight Says*, London: Faber, 1998.

Waterman, Andrew. 'Big Sprawl', *London Magazine*, December/January 1999–2000.

Wright, John M. 'Lyricism in Contemporary Australian Poetry', *Westerly*, Vol. 19, No. 4, 4 December 1974.

Zwicky, Fay. 'Language or Speech? A Colonial Dilemma', *Overland*, Vol. 98, April 1985.

GENERAL BOOKS

Anderson, Benedict. *Imagined Communities: Reflections on the Origin and Spread of Nationalism*, London: Verso, 1983; revised edition, 1991.

Ashcroft, Bill, Griffiths, Gareth, and Tiffin, Helen. *The Empire Writes Back: Theory and Practice in Postcolonial Literatures*, London: Routledge, 1989.

Barnes, John (ed.). *The Writer in Australia: A Collection of Literary*

Documents 1856 to 1964, Melbourne: Oxford University Press, 1969.

Bennett, Bruce. *Cross Currents: Magazines and Newspapers in Australian Literature*, Melbourne: Longman Cheshire, 1981.

—— *An Australian Compass*, South Fremantle: Fremantle Arts Centre Press, 1991.

Boehmer, Elleke. *Colonial and Postcolonial Literature*, Oxford: Oxford University Press, 1995.

—— (ed.). *Empire Writing*, Oxford: Oxford University Press, 1998.

Bolton, Geoffrey. *The Oxford History of Australia, Volume 5: 1942–1988, The Middle Way*, Melbourne: Oxford University Press, 1990.

Carter, Paul. *The Road to Botany Bay: An Essay in Spatial History*, London: Faber, 1987.

—— *Living in a New Country: History, Travelling and Language*, London: Faber, 1992.

—— *The Lie of the Land*, London: Faber, 1996.

Clark, Manning. *History of Australia*, London: Pimlico, 1993.

Coleman, Deirdre and Otto, Peter (eds). *Imagining Romanticism: Essays on English and Australian Romanticisms*, West Cornwall, CT: Locust Hill Press, 1992.

Darian-Smith, Kate, Gunner, Liz and Nuttall, Sarah (eds). *Text, Theory, Space: Land, Literature and History in South Africa and Australia*, London: Routledge, 1996.

—— and Hamilton, Paula. *Memory and History in Twentieth-Century Australia*, Oxford: Oxford University Press, 1994.

Docker, John. *In a Critical Condition: Reading Australian Literature*, Ringwood: Penguin, 1984.

Dutton, Geoffrey. *The Innovators: The Sydney Alternatives in the Rise of Modern Art, Literature and Ideas*, South Melbourne: Macmillan, 1986.

Elliott, Brian. *The Landscape of Australian Poetry*, Melbourne: Chesire, 1967.

—— *The Jindyworobaks*, St Lucia: University of Queensland Press, 1979.

Gelder, Ken and Jacobs, Jane M. (eds). *Uncanny Australia: Sacredness and Identity in a Postcolonial Nation*, Melbourne: Melbourne University Press, 1998.

Gibson, Ross. *The Diminishing Paradise: Changing Literary Perspectives of Australia,* Sydney: Sirius, 1984.

—— *South of the West: Postcolonialism and the Narrative Construction of Australia,* Bloomington: Indiana University Press, 1992.

Goodwin, Ken. *A History of Australian Literature,* London: Macmillan, 1986.

Gray, Robert and Lehmann, Geoffrey (eds). *The Younger Australian Poets,* Sydney: Hale and Iremonger, 1983.

Hall, Rodney and Shapcott, Thomas W. *New Impulses in Australian Poetry,* Queensland: University of Queensland Press, 1968.

Haskell, Dennis (ed.). *Kenneth Slessor,* Queensland: University of Queensland Press, 1991.

Hergenhan, Laurie (ed.). *The Penguin New Literary History of Australia,* Ringwood: Viking Penguin, 1988.

Hodge, Bob and Mishra, Vijay. *The Dark Side of the Dream: Australian Literature and the Postcolonial Mind,* London: Allen and Unwin, 1991.

Jordan, Richard and Pierce, Peter. *The Poet's Discovery,* Melbourne: Melbourne University Press, 1990.

Kiernan, Brian. *The Most Beautiful Lies,* Sydney: Angus and Robertson, 1977.

Kirkby, Joan (ed.). *The American Model: Influence and Independence in Australian Poetry,* Sydney: Hale and Iremonger, 1972.

Kramer, Leonie (ed.). *The Oxford History of Australian Literature,* Melbourne: Oxford University Press, 1981.

Lawson, Henry. *The Penguin Henry Lawson Short Stories,* John Barnes (ed.), Ringwood: Penguin, 1986.

Lazarus, Neil. *Nationalism and Cultural Practice in the Postcolonial World,* Cambridge: Cambridge University Press, 1999.

Loomba, Ania. *Colonialism/Postcolonialism,* London: Routledge, 1998.

McAuley, James. *A Map of Australian Verse,* Melbourne: Oxford University Press, 1975.

—— *The Grammar of the Real,* Melbourne: Melbourne University Press, 1975.

McDonald, Roger. *Gone Bush,* Sydney: Bantam, 1990.

McKernan, Susan. *A Question of Commitment: Australian Literature in the Twenty Years After the War,* Sydney: Allen and Unwin, 1989.

McLaren, John. *Writing in Hope and Fear: Literature as Politics in Postwar Australia*, Cambridge: Cambridge University Press, 1996.

Rutherford, Anna (ed.). *Aboriginal Culture Today*, Sydney: Dangeroo, 1988.

Schaffer, Kay. *Women and the Bush: Forces of Desire in Australian Culture*, Cambridge: Cambridge University Press, 1988.

Taylor, Andrew. *Reading Australian Poetry*, Queensland: University of Queenland Press, 1987.

Tiffin, Chris and Lawson, Alan (eds). *De-Scribing Empire: Postcolonialism and Textuality*, London: Routledge, 1994.

Ward, Russel. *The Australian Legend*, Melbourne: Oxford University Press, 1978.

White, Richard. *Inventing Australia: Images and Identity 1688-1980*, Sydney: George Allen & Unwin, 1981.

Wilkes, G.A. *The Stockyard and the Croquet Lawn: Literary Evidence for Australian Cultural Development*, London: Edward Arnold, 1981.

Wright, Judith. *Preoccupations in Australian Poetry*, Melbourne: Oxford University Press, 1965.

Index

Note: 'n' after a page refereance indicates a note number on that page

Printed in the United Kingdom by
Lightning Source UK Ltd., Milton Keynes
141048UK00001B/46/P